# THE BEST OF ZVI

# THE BEST OF ZVI:

## FIFTY YEARS TELLING THE STORY ON THE HIGHWAYS AND BYWAYS OF ISRAEL

By
Zvi Kalisher

Edited by
Amy Julian

The Friends of Israel
Gospel Ministry, Inc.
P. O. Box 908, Bellmawr, NJ 08099

**THE BEST OF ZVI:**
FIFTY YEARS TELLING THE STORY
ON THE HIGHWAYS AND BYWAYS OF ISRAEL

Copyright © 1998 by The Friends of Israel Gospel Ministry, Inc.,
P. O. Box 908, Bellmawr, NJ 08099
**Third Printing**...................................................................2014

Kalisher, Zvi

Editor: Amy Julian

Printed in the United States of America
Library of Congress Catalog Card Number: 98-073208
ISBN 13: 978-0-915540-59-4
ISBN 10: 0-915540-59-2

Visit our website at www.foi.org

# TABLE OF CONTENTS

Son of man, I have made thee a watchman unto the house of Israel; therefore,
hear the word at my mouth, and give
them warning from me. When I say unto
the wicked, Thou shalt surely die; and
thou givest him not warning, nor speakest
to warn the wicked from his wicked way,
to save his life, the same wicked man shall
die in his iniquity; but his blood will I
require at thine hand.  Yet if thou warn
the wicked, and he turns not from his
wickedness, nor from his wicked way, he
shall die in his iniquity; but thou hast
delivered thy soul.

Ezekiel 3:17-19

# FOREWORD

Early in 1948, a teenage Jewish war waif from Poland disembarked from a ship in Haifa, Israel. He had weathered the worst that the Holocaust could deliver: a ravished country, a lost childhood, and the death of his family. He had seen the ugliness of war in ways few have ever experienced. Little did he know, however, that what awaited him in his new home—Israel—would bring additional battle scars, as he and his people struggled for survival. But the physical pain and deprivation Zvi had endured were only a bleak covering for what was going on inside his tortured soul. Zvi desperately needed a friend. And, as chronicled in the biography of his life, *ZVI*, he found more than a friend when he received a new life in the Messiah, Jesus.

What has transpired over the ensuing fifty years is the history of a man who no longer wears Israeli army fatigues, but moves through the streets of Jerusalem in another uniform—the full armor of God.

For five decades, stories of his spiritual encounters have enriched lives and encouraged countless thousands of believers the world over. Now, through the efforts of our Managing Editor, Amy Julian, a selection of the best of Zvi's reports (which appear in each issue of *Israel My Glory*) has been compiled in book form. They cover the years from 1959 through 1998. As you read this book, you will meet a parade of people from all walks of life in Israel. Above all, you will thrill at what God continues to do through the life of this extraordinary man.

—Elwood McQuaid

## A LITTLE BLACK BOOK
## (ZVI'S TESTIMONY)

Following the War of Independence, Zvi left Haifa with a treasure tucked under his arm.  He had picked up a copy of the
Bible written in Hebrew.  It would, he figured, meet two primary
needs.  First, he could learn the answers to some of his questions
about God.  Second, it would be a great tool in helping him with
his mastery of Hebrew.

Back in Jerusalem, he spent many hours with his new source
of information.  Whenever he could persuade one of his companions to share some tent time assisting him with his reading pro-
gram, he was a happy man.  Soldiers had an abundance of time on
their hands now, and consequently it wasn't too difficult to find a
temporary tutor.

One afternoon he was puzzling his way through the Psalms when he
came across a statement that brought him to attention:  "When my
father and my mother forsake me, then the LORD will take me up.  Teach
me thy way, O LORD, and lead me in a plain path…" (Ps. 27:10-11).

"Who said this?" he asked the Sabra who had been chosen teacher for the day.

"King David," said his young comrade. "He was the second king of our nation. It was he who came here and made Jerusalem the royal city of Israel."

"If he was a king, living in a palace, why would he say a thing like this?" Zvi wondered.

"Very simple," said his instructor. "He was a king, yes, but a man with many troubles. He had great enemies from whom he was forced to flee. At one time even his son turned against him. Many of the things he wrote in the Psalms were about his times of trouble."

This David, Zvi concluded, was a man after his own heart—trouble upon trouble. Maybe he could learn something from a man who had spent time in the same boat as the maturing Jew from Poland.

Zvi's mother and father had forsaken him too. Of course, it was something over which they had no control, and he had nothing but love for and fond memories of them. Nevertheless, he had known the life of a forsaken waif, alone and surrounded by a host of enemies.

This man David said, when it had happened to him, that the Lord picked him up. Then he asked God to teach him and lead him in a plain path. It seemed astonishing to Zvi that one who lived so long ago could feel exactly as he did now. From now on, he determined, his prayer would be the same—that God would teach him and lead him in a plain path.

Zvi's tent home was something less than palatial, so he packed his belongings, folded his tent for the last time, and set out for new quarters at Talpiyot. The settlement center was located on the Bethlehem side of Jerusalem in an area that had been settled by Jews in 1924.

She came to Talpiyot after he had been there about two months. She was obviously a European—from Switzerland, he was to learn. Zvi judged by her looks that she was in her early sixties. The woman carried a bag full of little black books. He was seated outside his barrack home when she came by. The two of them shared a few minutes of pleasant conversation before she reached into her bag. "I would like to give you a book," she said.

"What kind of book is it?" Zvi asked.

"This is a New Testament written in Hebrew," she answered cheerfully.

"And what is a New Testament?" he queried.

"It is part of the Bible," she explained. "It will tell you about the Messiah."

He had heard references to the Messiah in his ghetto days in Europe and from religious Jews in the army. "I have heard something about the Messiah but know little beyond the name."

"Then this book will answer your questions," the woman told him earnestly. "There is only one stipulation in my giving it to you: You must promise that you will read it."

"Yes, I will be glad to read it," he promised.

"Read slowly," the woman said, "and ask the Lord to lead you to understand what you read."

Zvi accepted the little black book with words of gratitude.

When the woman was gone, he thought about what she had counseled him to do. "Ask the Lord to lead you to understand what you read." This is what he had read in the Psalm where David asked the Lord to lead him. The woman's words struck a chord in Zvi's spirit.

Zvi had read magazines in the past, and from time to time novels had fallen into his hands. He found, however, little to interest him in these volumes. The Swiss woman's little black book was another story. As the youthful searcher began to work his way through its pages, he found that it breathed with a vibrancy he had never encountered in a book before. Many of the quotations and references were somewhat familiar to him from what he had read in the Hebrew Bible he had picked up in Haifa. This book spoke about many places in Israel that were known to him. The stories and lessons of the Gospels began to give him answers to some of his questions, and his reading gave rise to a great many more questions.

Before long, his hunger for the content of his most precious possession began to approximate the drive he had long felt to know God. Zvi had no explanation for the way he felt. Yet he was intensely aware that this book drew him to it like a magnet. After awhile, he began to leave the busy and distracting atmosphere of the crowded camp to seek out the quiet parks of Jerusalem. There he would sit for hours, glued to the book.

Central in his thoughts was Jesus. The woman had told him this book would speak to him about the Messiah. It didn't take long for him to recognize whom his little book identified as that distinguished personage. Jesus of Nazareth intrigued him. He was thoroughly captivated by the unfolding of the Carpenter's life on the pages before him.

Above everything, he was impressed with the troubles Jesus encountered. This man did nothing but good, yet some men hated and opposed Him. Later they succeeded in nailing Him to a cross. He found it difficult to comprehend why this would happen. When he considered it carefully, he thought about how his own people—and he himself—had suffered without a reason.

One day, a friend discovered what he was reading and said, "That is not a book for Jews. It is just fairy tales and bluffs made up by Christians."

Zvi was puzzled. "I have read this book for many days now, and I admit that there is much about it I do not understand, but I have not read anything that has done me harm or caused me to want to become a bad person. I have read only good things in this book."

Wherever he went and whatever he was doing, his little black book was with him. He was afraid to leave it behind in his room for fear someone would take it. Whenever he had a few minutes, he could be found off to himself carefully perusing the open pages before him. Without a hand to guide him or a human voice to counsel him, he stayed close to the book that he somehow knew held the answers to his longings.

It was a sunny Wednesday evening. As Zvi returned to Talpiyot from his day's work in Jerusalem, he passed a small building. He could hear the sound of people lifting hearty voices in song. The words that came to his ears were from a hymn telling of the person about whom he had been reading—Jesus. Although it was not obvious from the external appearance of the building, he knew it must be a meeting of believers in Christ as Messiah.

For the next few evenings, he arranged his routine so he would be in that vicinity at the same time. He saw no life around the place until Sunday night, when once again he saw people filing into the building.

"Dare I enter?" he asked himself.

The following Wednesday evening, he did. There was singing, prayer, Bible reading, and the pastor spoke at length about verses that told of Jesus' prayer for His disciples and His love and concern for His people.

He returned the next Sunday, and the message was different. The pastor spoke of Jesus as the Sinbearer, the one who came as a substitute and took the sins of people on Himself, making it possible for men and women to be saved from their sins. "People," he said, "must turn from their sins and accept what the Messiah has done for them. We must be delivered from our sins by the sacrifice provided by the Messiah, Jesus."

The talk squared with the general concept Zvi had formed in his mind regarding the Messiah. For sometime to come, he came faithfully to the services.

But one Wednesday night Zvi left the service feeling depressed. He couldn't understand what was happening to him. Then, slowly, it came to him. He needed to do something about what he had heard and read—Zvi needed to be saved from his sin. That was it! That was what had made him feel so miserable. For awhile now, he had heard about the Messiah—words that agreed perfectly with what he had read in the Bible—but he had not done anything about it.

The next Wednesday night, he asked to speak with the pastor after the service. Following a long discussion, Zvi said, "It comes down to this: I want you to explain to me what I have to do to be saved."

The pastor was more than happy to answer all of his questions about Jesus, his own sin, and his need for a Savior. Then he asked, "Do you believe in Jesus as the Messiah, and are you willing to accept Him as your Savior and Lord?"

"Yes! Yes! Without any question," said Zvi, "I am convinced that He is the Messiah and my Savior."

The two men prayed together, and the simple transaction was completed—simple, yet profound beyond anything that can be computed or communicated through human phraseology. Zvi, survivor of the Holocaust, had experienced the new birth. Since boyhood, he had longed for and sought after a new beginning—now he had found it. He was a new creation in Jesus the Messiah.

—Excerpts from the book *ZVI*
by Elwood McQuaid

## INTO THE FIERY FURNACE

L ast Monday, a Christian brother and I went into what you might call a *fiery furnace*, seeking to bring the quenching waters of the gospel. We ventured into Mea Shearim, the center of the Ultra-Orthodox Jewish sect. How deep in darkness and sin these people are, in spite of their piety and religious fanaticism!

As we entered into a conversation, I read to a number of bystanders several passages from the Old and New Testaments, particularly stressing Leviticus 17:11, "it is the blood that maketh an atonement for the soul," and 1 John 1:7, "But if we walk in the light, as he is in the light, we have fellowship one with another, and the blood of Jesus Christ, his Son, cleanseth us from all sin."

When they heard this, they wanted to attack us, but we were not afraid for we knew that the Lord was with us. In the past, when I was in the Israeli army, I had frequent dealings with the younger generation of these Ultra-Orthodox people. At that time they called me "Goy" (*Gentile*) because I was not able to speak Yiddish. Now, however, I distribute Hebrew tracts and tell them about the Lord

Jesus Christ, who shed His blood that we might have eternal life. I am also able to speak to them in Yiddish, which I have learned here in Jerusalem.

These Ultra-Orthodox Jews refuse to speak Hebrew because they consider it "the holy language" to be used only for prayer in the synagogue.

As I witnessed to them, I told them that the only way out of the present darkness is through the blood of the Lamb. When they heard this, their faces became livid with anger. I then said to my companion, "Now is the time to get out of here, or they will liquidate us."

The interesting thing is that none of them threw away the pamphlets we gave them or returned them to us. Praise the Lord for that!

I remember how your worker, Rachel, used to go out into this section of Jerusalem to proclaim the Word of God and His plan of salvation. Sometimes she would come back with black eyes, her face marred beyond recognition, and her clothing torn. Although she suffered a great deal at the hands of these zealots, she did not tell anyone about it. When I questioned her about it, she would only say, "Those who suffer for the Lord here on earth will have eternal life with Him in heaven."

—1959

# A FISH STORY—THAT WAS TRUE!

I recently visited a settlement in the Negev wilderness to distribute the Bibles you sent. How grateful these people were to receive the Word of God.

While waiting for our group to gather, I had a wonderful opportunity to get to know these people better. Some of them had never owned a Bible of their own. How happy they were to be able to read, each in his or her own Bible.

Among those who came to the meeting was a new visitor who objected to my reading from the New Testament. I therefore read portions from the Old Testament as well as from the New. This took about two hours. In the end, the visitor was satisfied, and we were able to carry on our Bible meeting in a brotherly fashion. He was no longer hostile but listened carefully.

Then we prayed together, and I again read Ezekiel 33, Jeremiah 29, and other passages from both the Old and New Testaments. It was the first time in my life that I had conducted such a long meeting. Lunch time passed, and then supper time—but I did not realize it.

These people are refugees from behind the Iron Curtain, and they have never heard about the Bible except for the lies that the Communists have told them. It was wonderful to give them the Word of God. Our new friend also promised to attend our next meeting.

By the time I left the settlement, it was late Friday evening and the Sabbath had already begun. As the buses were no longer running, I started walking back to my home in Jerusalem. After I had walked about four miles, a military truck came along, and the driver gave me a lift to Ain Karem, the birthplace of John the Baptist, which is about four miles from Jerusalem. By this time it was 10:30 p.m. I then walked the rest of the way to Jerusalem, arriving home before midnight. Strangely, I did not feel tired but was inwardly excited and very happy.

When at last I arrived home, my wife asked, "Where have you been all day?" I told her that I had gone fishing. She did not understand what I meant, so I explained to her what kind of *fishing* I had done—*fishing for souls.*

—1960

## ZVI IS WOUNDED

Recently I spent some time in the hospital as a result of a wound in the hand received during the Arab-Israel border disturbances. Truly, the Lord was on my side and saved me; however, I lost a great deal of blood while under fire. In the hospital, they gave me many blood transfusions, and after a week I felt much better.

During my stay in the hospital, I had the opportunity to witness to other Israeli soldiers. As I read my Hebrew Bible aloud, they asked me if I went to a rabbinical school. I replied, "I do not, but I am a believer in God and also in His only begotten Son, who gives us eternal life through faith in Him."

Many of the boys did not understand what I was saying, but I had plenty of time on my hands, so I could go into some detail and explain to them the Old Testament. It was a great pity that I did not have a New Testament with me. You see, during the action I lost all of my personal belongings. I had only the Bible that the military rabbinate gives to every soldier.

What a shame that these boys do not understand what they read.

I can only tell you that I am not in the least bit sorry that I had to go to the hospital, as it gave me the opportunity to tell the "good news" to so many. Every day we had long discussions. That made me forget about my pain. When the physicians came in, they joined in the discussions. The nurses said, "All of a sudden the soldiers have become theologians. What is the matter with them?"

Now I am home again. My wife expects our first baby soon, and she was very concerned about me. I had to conceal my pain so that I would not add to her worry. But the Lord has given me much endurance, and I do not care about physical suffering.

Since my return from the hospital, I have been able to visit some of our believing friends and their families. We pray together, and they always remember you. I hope that soon I will be able to return to work.

—1960

## ZVI IS IN THE HOSPITAL AGAIN—
## AS AN EMPLOYEE AND A WITNESS

R ecently I found work in a Jerusalem hospital as a handyman.
The day after I started working there, something happened that
was a clear sign of the Lord's guidance.

When I walked into one of the wards to repair a window, I saw a
Polish Jew, a man about 50 years of age who has been in Israel for 35
years. He was in critical condition, and I felt led to witness to him in
my spare time so that he might receive Christ before his death.

The man told me the tragic story of how his family had been
killed during the Arab pogrom in 1930 in the city of Hebron.

"When my family perished," he said, "I was left alone, a teenage
boy. I soon got into bad company with a gang of Arabs who smug-
gled morphine across the border. It was risky work, but they paid
me well. However, in a short time I became a victim of my sordid
trade. I became addicted to the dope I was smuggling and would
do anything to get it because I could not live without it. Seeing my
condition, my companions took advantage of me and sent me on

the most dangerous assignments, mostly to Egypt and Lebanon. One day the British police caught me, and I was imprisoned for a year, desperately sick and craving morphine.

"After my release from prison, I had nowhere to go, so I returned to my old gang in Jaffa. They received me gladly and assigned me a new job. They bought camels from Bedouins and instructed me to drive the animals across the border into Egypt. At first, I could not understand why they were doing this, but I soon learned the reason. They were inserting in each camel's stomach 15 bottles of morphine worth about $4,500. The cost of a camel was only about $25 to $30. When I took the camels to Egypt, their Egyptian partner would pay the high price of the morphine and kill the poor animals right away, leaving their flesh to rot.

"By now I had enough money to indulge in my vice. But I was caught again and handed over to a British court in Jerusalem. The judge was Jewish. I confessed everything and told him about my partners in crime. He sentenced me to three years in prison. Altogether, I have spent 19 years of my life in prison.

"And now," he finished his tragic tale, "I am on my deathbed, and no one cares to speak even a word to me to relieve my anxious soul. You are the first person interested enough to hear me out."

I told him that I believe in the living God, the Judge of the living and the dead, and that because He loves us, He sent His only Son to save sinners such as he and I. I read to him from the Gospel of Luke, chapter 19, the story of Zacchaeus and the Son of Man who came to seek and to save those who are lost. I also read Jesus' promise that because He lives, we will also live (Jn. 10:10), along with many other Scripture passages. I said, "It is obvious that your time is short, and you cannot afford to waste any of it."

All of a sudden the poor man broke down, crying, and said, "I am unworthy of anyone telling me about God and His salvation." I told him, "Christ died for sinners, that they may have eternal life.

It is up to you to receive the Lord Jesus as your Savior, so that you may have that eternal life. This may be your last opportunity."

He then said, "Please pray for me," which I did. Then he looked at me and said, "Now I am ready to receive the Lord." He was very weak, but I was sure that he truly believed. I asked "Do you believe that Jesus is your Savior?" In a soft voice, he answered, "Yes, and I am ready to be with the Lord Jesus. I am no longer afraid because I will go home to Him." When I said goodbye, His last words to me were, "You saved my life."

The next morning, when I returned to work at the hospital, I was told that during the night my friend had gone to his eternal home.

—1961

## IF THIS IS POISON....

I recently had some strange visitors in my home quite unexpectedly. They were four men with long beards and side locks. They greeted me pleasantly, and I invited them in and asked them to be seated at the table. At first they hesitated. Then one of them said, "It has come to our ears that you are spreading poison among the *righteous ones* [pious Jews]." I replied, "I never carry any poison with me. But if you are speaking of the Word of God, I plead guilty because I do distribute the Scriptures. No one can forbid me to do this because I am a citizen of Israel and have fought as a soldier for Israel's independence. I am still in my country's service, and no one can forbid me to believe in Christ. I do not force anyone to believe in the Messiah, but I try as best I can to explain to people the reason why I believe, and I encourage them to read the Scriptures.

"If this is poison, then what do you believe?" I asked them in turn. They looked at me as if I were a wolf. When they realized that I was not afraid of them, they asked me the reason for my faith. I told them, "I have read the prophets and the other Scriptures, as well as the New Testament, and have come to the conviction that there is one God, and He came down to this earth in the form of a man to take our sins upon Himself. He was crucified, died, was buried, and rose again from the dead. It is by faith in Him that we receive eternal life." When they heard this, their ears went up like a hare's, and they looked at me in bewilderment.

Just then my wife came in with a tray of tea and cookies and invited them very courteously to partake of the refreshments. They found it awkward to refuse, so they sat down at the table and drank tea and ate cookies.

By now I thought that they had had enough discussion. But no—as soon as they finished their tea, they started all over again.

The eldest man made me a proposition: "If you stop preaching the gospel, we will give you a good job and help you in other ways." I replied, "My soul is not for sale!" I went on to tell them, "Here in Israel, we live under a democratic form of government, and no one can forbid a citizen to believe what he wants to or to distribute the Word of God."

I also told them, "There were others like you in the past—for instance, a man named Saul, who went about in the synagogues speaking against the Lord Jesus. One day he met Jesus, and his eyes were opened. He became His greatest apostle and was known as Paul."

At this point they thanked us for our friendly reception and promised to come again shortly. I pray that when they come, the Lord will open their eyes that they will see the truth.

Our little Ruth, who will soon be a year old, is beginning to talk. She says, "Abba"—Daddy.

—1961

## SITTING ON TOP OF A VOLCANO

First, I want to give you the happy news that my wife recently gave birth to our second son, We are going to call him Victor [after Victor Buksbazen, the first Director of The Friends of Israel]. We are pleased that he has joined his older sister and brother, Ruth and Meno.

I was called up for military service recently, and this time it was a miracle that I came home alive. I thank God that I was saved from this *boiling pot*, which is impossible to describe. It is like a volcano that erupts every few months. By now, I have become used to it.

After this trip, I visited a family whose two oldest children had recently married. Now there are only six children left at home, the oldest being 14 and the youngest three. I visited their home in the company of my commanding officer, and they received us courteously. This officer treats me very well, although he knows that I am a believer. A year ago he took my New Testament from my rucksack, and we are now great friends. Because of his position, he has to be very careful. The authorities cannot do anything to me, but he has rank and could get himself into trouble.

We were able to discuss the things of Christ in the home of the family we visited. We prayed together, and they thanked me for visiting them again.

When I returned to my work, my fellow-laborers could not believe that I had come back. One of them said, "A goy has luck." (They call me a *goy—Gentile*—because I believe in Jesus.) He said, "Couldn't you have gotten killed, instead of one of our own?" I answered, "Is it perhaps because the Lord has a plan for me—to proclaim His gospel— that He saved me? I am sure of this. And this is not the first time that the Lord has saved me. I have been in similar situations before, but, as you can see, I am safe and sound. Is it not a miracle?"

My foreman stood on the sidelines listening to our conversation, and at the end he came to me and said, "If you do not stop these communications about the gospel, I will dismiss you." I answered, "If you wish, you can do so immediately, but I will say what I want to say, and no one can forbid me. I am not employed here as a high official, but as a hard-working construction man. What is your decision?" He thought for a moment and then said, "Stay." "I take it then," I said, "that you really enjoy hearing my testimony and that I am permitted to say what I stand for?"

This incident gave me greater courage to bear witness every time I can, whenever I can, and wherever I can. Most of the people with whom I work are from Kurdistan and Iraq and have never before heard about the Lord Jesus. That is why the foreman was so afraid of my testimony. But, whether he likes it or not, he hears about the Lord. I do my work well, and he can find no fault with me. I said to him, "The day will come when you will implore the Lord, in the name of Jesus, to forgive you. There are no heroes before God." He replied, "Enough of the lesson for today." I then remarked, "I would like you, not only to learn the lesson, but to do some homework." For the first time, he laughed. Now the men who work with me are very interested and ask me many questions.

—1965

## LET'S MAKE A DEAL

Most of my fellow construction workers are pious Jews. During one recent lunch hour, they were discussing the question of who will have a share in the life to come. Knowing that some of them are very fanatical, I stayed out of their conversation. One of them, however, said to me, "You can in no way have a share in the life to come because you are an apostate who believes in Jesus."

The foreman heard it and was very pleased that I was attacked, but this did not spoil my appetite. One of the men said to me, "Let's make a deal. You give me your good deeds, and I will pay you money for them. Since you are a *meshumad* (*traitor*), you do not need your good deeds because they will not admit you to eternal life. But I can use your good deeds. In this way, I will make certain of my share in eternal life."

In answer, I told him, "I have a much better way of obtaining eternal life, and I will share it with you. Here is a complete Bible, including the New Testament, and, as an introduction, I recommend that you read Isaiah 61:1-2." I then decided to read the passage for him: "The Spirit of the Lord GOD is upon me, because the LORD hath anointed me to preach good tidings unto the meek; he hath sent me to bind up the brokenhearted, to proclaim liberty to the captives, and the opening of the prison to those who are bound; To proclaim the acceptable year of the LORD, and the day of vengeance of our God; to comfort all that mourn."

When I finished reading, several of the men attacked me physically. I did not reciprocate but said, "You are fortunate that I am a believer in Jesus. My Lord has told me that we should show love to those who hate us because, by nature, I am a human being just like you, with a very heavy hand. If I have any 'good deeds,' it is only by faith in the living God and in the Messiah. This is the only way that assures people of eternal life."

The foreman said, "Jesus was crucified long ago, and his death does not make any difference to anyone." I replied, "We who believe in Him know that He was not only crucified but that He rose again and lives in our hearts. We feel His presence every day, all day long. I recommend Him to you. Then you also will know differently and feel differently."

The foreman became excited and said, "You need not come back to work tomorrow. Let's see if your Messiah will help you now." The next morning, I turned up at my job, as usual, and the foreman never said a word. A week later he asked, "Did your Messiah help you yet?" "Indeed He did!" I replied. "He gave me my job." "Where?" he asked. "Right here!" I replied.

I remembered the words of our Lord: "Blessed are ye, when men shall revile you, and persecute you, and shall say all manner of evil against you falsely, for my sake. Rejoice, and be exceedingly glad; for great is your reward in heaven; for so persecuted they the prophets who were before you" (Mt. 5:11-12).

—1966

## MOST DANGEROUS WORK

Our third son, little David, is now quite a big fellow. He suffered a great deal during the war, as did the other children—Ruth, Meno, and Victor—along with my wife. As soon as she returned home from the hospital after giving birth to David, she had to go to an air raid shelter and take care of our four young children in very confined quarters, while I went away to war. But, thank God, that is in the past. The older children prayed while in the shelter, "Lord, send back our Daddy to us in health," and the Lord answered the prayers of these little ones. I returned safely.

There is much work for me on the front, as the Arabs have sown many land mines, and they add more each night. I have to defuse these mines, and it is most dangerous work. Of the 30 men who started in our group, only three remain. A person must have a great deal of patience and nerves of steel to do this kind of work, and the Lord has given these to me and has spared me. The men who work with me respect me greatly. I am their instructor and teach them how to disarm the mines.

It makes me very unhappy to see my friends being killed or wounded regularly in this work. I visit my pupils in the hospital or at their graves. If they are wounded, I give them my testimony and seek to comfort them as best I can. The war is not over yet, and we shall have many more sacrifices. Every day I thank God for sparing me for yet a while longer.

When I get into this work, I forget myself and just think about the others around me, trying to help them. Some have said to me, "How can you, a Christian, fight in a war? Doesn't Jesus say that if your enemy smites you on one cheek, give him the other?" I always reply, "You must remember that I am here as a citizen who has been called up by the government to defend my country. The war is not my choice at all." I also tell them about the Lord's answer to the Pharisees, who asked Him whether they should pay a tax. He showed them a coin bearing Caesar's image and said, "Render, therefore, unto Caesar the things which are Caesar's; and unto God, the things that are God's" (Mt. 22:21). As a citizen, I must fulfill my obligations. I try to make my life and service a testimony, forgetting myself and helping others, even at the risk of my own life. I think this is a testimony for the Lord.

I have tried to get a transfer to another company, but they will not permit it. They say, "Only old age or death will release you. We need you too much." They even cited me for an award, although financially the situation is very bad. I barely make enough to feed my family. Still, I am not ashamed of the Lord Jesus Christ, my Savior, and I witness for Him wherever I can. Even if I have to suffer and die, I know that I will have eternal life with Him.

—1968

## WHAT DO YOU THINK OF THE MESSIAH?

The situation in Israel is very tense. There is no peace. Most of the time I am on duty and must patrol the dark streets of Jerusalem on the Arab side. My task is to look for mines and booby traps. I must watch my step all the time.

Our neighboring Arab countries continually threaten to destroy us, but we are not afraid and trust in the Lord. We must hold on to this land; otherwise, they shall drive us into the sea. The Lord has promised this land to our people, and there is no power on earth that can gainsay the Lord's will. In the meantime, I give my testimony concerning our Messiah and Savior to as many people as possible. I have visited many friends, witnessing to them, because we do not know what the next day will bring.

Last Thursday, I was on patrol in the main street of former Arab Jerusalem. Around three o'clock in the morning, I noticed a group of people coming my way. They were fully dressed in black robes. I thought they were priests, but when they came close I realized that they were students at an Orthodox Jewish school. Because it was my duty to do so, I stopped them and asked what they were doing out so early in the morning. They answered in unison, "We are going to the West Wall to recite *Slichot*" (penitential prayers usually recited before New Year and the Day of Atonement).

At first they were frightened, but when they saw that I was an Israeli soldier, they took courage. I asked, "When do you think the Temple will be rebuilt? Why don't you start now, since you have the Wailing Wall in your possession?" One of them said, "Only when the Messiah comes will the Temple be rebuilt." "And where is the Messiah?" I asked. He answered, "He is already here, but He is waiting to make Himself manifest. He will build the Temple, and all the dead shall rise from their graves. We ourselves have no right to build the Temple. We are unclean and must not touch this work on the Holy Temple."

Their leader, who was a rabbi, asked, "What do you think of the Messiah, the son of David, soldier?" I answered, "The Messiah, the son of David, has come and is coming again. I know Him, and many other people know Him and have received Him as their Messiah and Savior. He laid down His life for our sins and made full atonement for us, according to Isaiah 53 and Psalm 22." I gave them many other Scriptures to make my point.

They stood there amazed, hearing things that apparently they did not know. The Lord Himself put the words into my mouth. Whatever the question, I gave them a scriptural answer. I was amazed at myself and realized that the Holy Spirit was guiding me. Usually Orthodox Jews do not talk to anyone who confesses Jesus as the Messiah, but they were most thrilled and impressed by the fact that I was a soldier guarding their safety while they are asleep or when they go to the Wailing Wall to pray. After I gave them my testimony, I asked, "Do you think I should have the same rights as any other Jewish person here in Israel? Or don't I deserve such rights?" The rabbi said, "You have asked a hard question, one that is difficult to answer." I insisted that he give me an answer because I wanted to know his opinion. "Well," he said, "if all the Jewish Christians were like you, we would have no difficulty at all."

Instead of going on to the Wailing Wall, they lingered around me and discussed the Messiah and messianic prophecies until nearly six o'clock in the morning. We hardly realized that the night had passed and the morning had arrived.

—1969

## HOW CAN YOU SLEEP?

I am in uniform again in a mountainous region where the winds blow fiercely. Down below we can see the place where Absalom, David's son, killed his brother, Amnon. In this country, vendettas can go on for years, and this is not just ancient history but a present-day reality. Today, however, they do not use daggers or swords but artillery and mines. This happens on both sides, night and day, and each side seems happy that it has done more harm to the other than they have received themselves. What will be the end of it? Only the Lord knows.

Some people lay awake at night thinking about these things, but I have gotten over it. Usually I have only two hours to sleep, so as soon as I hit the ground, I am dead to the world. They can shoot all the guns they have, but I have peace in my heart because I have a good protector, one whom few others have.

The other night, after I had slept a little while, someone awoke me. He was jealous that I could sleep during all the uproar. His eyes were almost glued together, and he asked, "How can you sleep at a time like this, with shells bursting all around us? Are you crazy? Have you no fear?"

Quoting Scripture, I said, "When I am afraid, I will trust in thee….in God I have put my trust; I will not fear what flesh can do unto me" (Ps. 56:3-4). I then told him, "One who has no faith must always be in fear. To be safe, you must trust God to take care of you and to watch over you. It is the same with sheep. If they do not have a good shepherd, they sense that they are without protection and they quiver. But when they feel that they have a good shepherd who watches over them, they feel secure and will lie down in the field and doze. My Lord said, 'I am the good shepherd, and know my sheep, and am known of mine' [Jn. 10:14]."

The man was very tired, but somehow, after I had spoken to him, his sleep left him and he asked, "What does this parable mean? What are you trying to tell me?"

I told him how the Messiah Jesus slept in the bottom of a boat on the Sea of Galilee while His disciples were almost out of their minds with fear because of the fierce storm and the huge waves raging around them. Being in terror, they woke Him, but He rebuked them, saying, "Why are ye fearful, O ye of little faith?" (Mt. 8:26).

I explained that I can sleep so soundly because I know that my Shepherd watches over me. "Trust in the Lord," I told him, "and go to sleep. In the morning we will talk further."

He then put his head down on the stones, which we call the "Hilton Hotel," and immediately went to sleep. He slept like the dead for two hours, while the shooting went on. It did not disturb him. In the morning we met again at the field kitchen. He left everything and came over to me, saying, "I slept like a child. What kind of psychology did you use on me? It certainly was effective. I do not understand what all this is about, but if it is going to do for me what it has done for you, then I am ready to believe as you do."

I then asked him, "What do you think is better—to walk against the wind or with the wind?" "With the wind, of course," he answered. "It is the same when you walk with the Lord," I explained. "You are never alone. He is always with you and gives you His strength. We are going through dangerous times now. Any moment might be the last for both of us. It would be terrible at such a time as this to deny the truth. How can a person reject the Lord, who has given us new life, new thoughts, and a wonderful future? He told us, 'Come unto me, all ye that labor and are heavy laden, and I will give you rest' [Mt. 11:28]. Is it not better to trust Him than to walk in fear and worry?"

The soldier took his soup from the kitchen and, sitting down beside me on a little knoll, he said quietly, "I thank God that He gave me comfort. I now feel as if I were home. Even the shooting does not bother me anymore. There must be some great power from above. I would not like to lose it because I can see what it has done for me. I pray that I will always have the same faith that I have now. What a fortunate man you are!"

We became fast friends and still share the same stone for a pillow. Wherever I go, my newfound friend tags along. He seems to be a different person. He has no fear and laughs and talks to me all the time.

—1969

# WITH AN ARAB FAMILY IN BETHLEHEM

A few days ago, I went to Bethlehem to visit an injured Arab friend who had worked with me on a building and had fallen from the scaffolding. All of his family and friends were there—about thirty people.

At first the conversation was about general matters, but then someone remarked, "When God created Eve, He deceived and desecrated Adam by putting him to sleep and robbing him of his rib to make a woman. Apparently, already back then God was on the side of the Jews." The logic of this statement did not make any sense to me. Soon the people became increasingly more excited, and I could not get in a word. Sensing their fanaticism and bitterness, I decided to leave, but the head of the house became quite hostile and prevented me from going.

I said, "I came here to visit a fellow worker who was injured on the job, and you treat me like this? Shame on you! This is not at all in the Arab tradition of hospitality to a guest!"

My words apparently had a sobering effect on them, especially when I said in Arabic, "God is one, and He is for all people without exception. He is for the Arabs, the Jews, and everybody else. When God created mankind, there were no Jews, no Arabs, no other nationalities. But when man sinned, he soon learned to hate others and to kill. People began to spread false rumors about each other and to despise each other. For instance, you have been told that Jewish people have horns and tails, but you live among us and can see with your own eyes that we are the same kind of people as you are. In fact, we are your relatives through Abraham. God promised him that through his seed there would come forth many nations. That promise was made before there were any Arabs or Jews. In the course of time, the children of Abraham began to hate and persecute one another. They forgot what it is to have mercy and compassion, until the time came when our Father in heaven sent His salvation into the world. And where did that happen? Right here in this little town of Bethlehem. Here was born the one whom you call *Isa*, and the Jews call *Yeshua*, and all the world knows as *Jesus*. This Jesus brought to all people forgiveness of sins and eternal salvation, and He taught us to love one another."

The eldest man present remarked, "How amazing! I thought the Jews hated Jesus, but you defend Him. Are you really a Jew?" I replied, "Yes. We who believe in Jesus are completed Jews. The reason I came to see you is because Jesus put love into my heart and told me to come and see you. Jesus told us to love our enemies."

One of the men said, "We all respect you for what you believe, but we cannot agree with one thing. This Isa [Jesus], as we believe, was a prophet, but Mohammed was the greatest of all prophets." I showed them from the Scriptures that the Lord Jesus Christ was the one promised in the Old Testament. I explained that the New Testament tells us how He brought love into the world, in contrast with the Koran, which (in Sura 190) says, "Hate your enemy, kill him wherever you find him." They looked at each other perplexed and could not answer me. I then read to them John 3:16: "For God so loved the world, that he gave his only begotten Son, that whosoever believeth in him should not perish, but have everlasting life."

Finally one man said, "The Jews are smarter than we Arabs." "No," I said, "this is not cleverness, but the wisdom and love of God. However, love cannot enter where there is darkness and bitter hatred."

The eldest man then began to cry. He walked over to me, embraced me, kissed me, and said, "Thank you very much. You taught us a great lesson today. We have so much to learn, especially about love. This is so strange to us."

—1971

## ZEAL WITHOUT KNOWLEDGE

Recently I worked at Mount Scopus, where a part of the University of Jerusalem is located. They are building new housing there for students.

At about 11 o'clock in the morning, an Orthodox student with a considerable beard approached me. He looked around, as if trying to find someone. I asked, "Can I help you?" He looked up and said, "Praise the Lord! I have been looking for Jews, but all of the workers here seem to be Arabs. I am so glad to have found at least one Jew. I would like you to do me a favor and help me." He was holding a package in his hand, and I asked, "What can I do for you?"

"The Passover holidays are approaching," he explained, "and the students do not even know what they are. *Shabbath Hagadol*, the Sabbath before the Passover, is already upon is. I have with me a package of *Agadoth le pesach* [the Passover story]. I would like you to distribute these booklets among the students."

I replied, "If you had Bibles for distribution, I would gladly hand them out for you. These booklets are a mixture of truth and legend that little children learn in their classes. The Bible, however, is the Word of God—wisdom for everyone."

He said, "You may be right, but Bibles are very expensive, and we cannot afford them." Then I made him an offer: "If you will pay for five complete Bibles, I will pay for five complete Bibles, and we will give them to the students." "What do you mean by a *complete* Bible?" he asked. I told him, "A *complete* Bible is the Old and New Testaments bound together."

He grabbed his head and exclaimed, "For more than an hour I have been looking for a Jew, and when I finally find one, he turns out to be a goy." I then showed him my order to report for military duty. When he read my full name, he said, "Yes, that is a fine Jewish name. What do you have to do with the New Testament? I am very curious."

I told him, "Years ago I knew nothing about the New Testament or Jesus. Then God, in His mercy, sent a New Testament my way, and now I love Jesus and seek to serve Him. Just because our forefathers went astray, that does not mean that I should follow in their footsteps and make the same mistakes they did. For the sake of my own soul, the souls of my children, and those of everyone else I meet, I must try to help people. Many may be looking for the truth without even knowing it, but they have no one to guide them. Isaiah 53:6 says, 'All we like sheep have gone astray; we have turned every one to his own way, and the LORD hath laid on him the iniquity of us all.' The prophet spoke about our Messiah, the one who paid the price of our redemption."

"You talk like a missionary," he said. "I must not listen to you because I cannot answer you. Now I see why there are so many of you."

"No," I replied, "it is not our doing, but the Lord Himself who works in the minds and hearts of people. His good seed germinates in the hearts of those who are sincere. All we have to do is water the seed and keep the weeds from choking the wheat. You too may become a new person through the Messiah Jesus."

"I must confess," he said, "that I cannot answer you now. What you say staggers me, but I am glad I met you." Do pray for this man.

—1971

## THE PEACEMAKER

Last week I had an extraordinary experience. As I was walking with my children in the Old City of Jerusalem, on the way to buy groceries, we passed an ice cream parlor. Little David asked me to buy him an ice cream cone, and naturally Ruth, Meno, and Victor wanted the same. And so, we went inside and bought the treats!

As the children were eating their ice cream, I noticed a man sitting at a table reading aloud the Psalms. I knew this man and realized that he was not the Psalm-reading type, so I asked him if someone in his family was sick (it is customary among Jewish people to read the Psalms when a family member is sick). "No," he replied, "no one in my family is sick."

He then led me into a back room, where I saw four men sitting at a table playing cards. Intrigued, I asked, "What does reading the Psalms have to do with playing cards?" He told me a sad and sordid story.

He was an habitual card player and had lost all his money. In desperation, he went to a so-called "wise man" for advice. This "wise man" counseled him to borrow more money and hire an expert card player to win back what he had lost. He therefore borrowed a considerable amount of money and even pawned his wife's gold watch, which he had given to her before their marriage. Then he started to recite the Psalms, thinking that would help him win back his money and his wife's gold watch. Soon, however, he had lost the borrowed money and the money received from the watch. Now he was ashamed and even afraid to go home. "What shall I do?" he asked in despair.

"First," I replied, "you must immediately stop playing cards or participating in any other form of gambling. Otherwise, you will suffer an even greater calamity. Then you must pray to God to give you a new heart and a new spirit." In his anxiety and embarrassment, he promised to do all that I had told him, but he begged me to go home with him, as he was ashamed and afraid of his wife and children.

After completing my shopping, I took my children home and then accompanied this man to his home. There I found his wife, distraught and very angry. The children looked hungry and dirty and lacked proper clothing and shoes. I spoke quietly to his wife and told her she should try and forgive him; otherwise, the situation would become even more desperate. Little by little, I managed to quiet her. Her husband wept and promised never to play cards again. But I told him, "Unless you accept the Messiah into your heart, you will never be able to keep that promise."

His wife then asked, "How can a decent man like you befriend such a wretch as my husband, whose sins weigh more than he himself?" I told her that our Savior came to heal those who were sick—people just like her husband.

"It is possible," I said, "that the Lord allowed him to get into this predicament so that he would realize his own helplessness. Perhaps God used me as His messenger to help him." After I left, the husband and wife were reconciled. A few days later he found a job.

Now he works at my side.

Last Sabbath, I went to this family's home and took them with me to our place of worship. After the service, I invited them to my home for dinner. Let us pray for the salvation of this family. The Lord is able.

—1972

## SADAT SUPPORTS
## THE JEWISH MISSIONARIES!

Here in Israel, people are making merry. It is Purim, and they are dancing in the streets. All daily problems seem to be forgotten for a while. All problems, that is, except the Hebrew-Christians. Recently the popular newspaper, *Yediot Achronot*, complained that Jewish high school students are interested in Jesus. The teachers, the paper said, made a big mistake allowing them to read the New Testament. "We must warn the teachers against the great calamity which the missionaries are preparing for us," the article stated.

In the same issue, the newspaper carried another article asserting that the missionaries are seeking to undermine the State of Israel. "They [the Hebrew-Christians] have no financial problems, because they get all the money they want from President Sadat of Egypt. And what is our government doing? Nothing! It just stands by and looks on while the missionaries are trying to destroy our nation. This is no longer a question of religion but of our survival." The newspaper asked, "Is there no way to deal with them?" People who were ill-disposed toward us in the past view such articles as a call to violence.

Yesterday, a man whom I know stopped me on the street and said, "You are one of those internal enemies." He wanted to fight me. I said to him, "Wait a moment. Maybe what you read isn't true at all. If you can prove that what you read about Jewish Christians is true, I will let you have my apartment with all the furniture, and it won't cost you a single penny. I will even help you move into it. You can have one week to prove that what the newspaper said about us is true. I will even make this promise in the presence of all your friends."

This appealed to him, and he could already see himself as the proud owner of a difficult-to-obtain apartment.

I went home with this man, who introduced me to his friends saying, "Here is one of those who believes in Yeshua." Then he told them what I had said to him. One of his friends asked, "And what if the whole story is untrue? Are you ready to pay Zvi compensation, say 50,000 Israeli pounds?" "Who, me?" he replied. "I can't do that. It would ruin me."

The same man then said to me, "If what the newspapers write about you Jewish believers is false, why don't you sue them in the courts for libel?" I replied, "My Savior died on a cross for my sins. He was put to death by His enemies, and yet He forgave them. Why should I sue people over a stupid newspaper article?"

They all laughed good-naturedly. Then I sat down and explained my faith to them. At the end of our conversation, the man who wanted to fight asked for my forgiveness. Then they all shook hands with me.

—1973

# I AM NOT ASHAMED OF HIM
# IN WHOM I BELIEVE!

When I returned home from the army recently, there was a surprise waiting for me—two ladies. I learned that they were from the *Aqudat Israel*, a fanatic Jewish group, and they were very angry.

"What do you wish of me?" I questioned. "We have come to save your family from death!" was their reply. "What death?" I asked. "Who wants to kill us?" "Jews," they replied. "We have heard about you, that you are a convert. We want to help you and your family. We want to save you."

"First," I began, "it is *you* who need salvation. I *am* saved, so you don't have to worry about me and my family. I am happy in my heart at what God has given me. Even if you sincerely want to do something for me, you cannot because you have no power. You are very weak in faith, so how can you help others? I am sure that God sent you to me so that you could be shown the way of salvation through our Lord, our Savior, who died on the cross and now lives.

Only through His power can you be saved, along with those who sent you. They are blind people."

"We are not here to listen to your missionary propaganda," they said. "You are also missionaries," I told them, "because you have come to me with your propaganda." "We are not missionaries. *You* are!" they exclaimed. "Yes, I am," I replied, "and I am not ashamed of Him in whom I believe. Even Abraham was a missionary, along with Jonah and the other prophets. Why am I, then, forbidden to be a missionary?"

The ladies threatened to have my position published in all the newspapers, saying that I am sowing poison against God in the Holy Land. I asked, "How do you know that I sow poison, and are you so holy and righteous?" They didn't answer me immediately, but finally one of them said, "If I could, I would kill you!"

I then opened the New Testament and read to her Romans 12:9-21, which tells of the Lord's love to us. "If you call this poison," I told her, "then I don't know what to say. I know that all the people to whom I speak about our Savior are alive. None of them has died; rather, they are happy because they have hope. They shall never die."

"If that is so," she threatened, "we will write about you, and then you will be sorry." "Never, never," I replied. Then I read Romans 8:38-39, telling her, "Not only will I read the Scriptures to you, but I am ready to face every obstacle you place in my path. I am not afraid."

"We are weak women," she said. "We will send our husbands to you; they are strong." "If you like," I said, "I will go with you to your homes—right now." "Aren't you afraid that our husbands will make trouble for you?" she asked. "No one can do me harm if it is not God's will," I insisted. "I'm ready, and I'm not afraid."

Then one woman asked the other, "What shall we do now?" They spoke Russian between themselves, not realizing that I know the Russian language very well. Continuing in Russian, one asked, "How can we go having done nothing? What should we say to him, for he is right?" "No, he is not right," the other insisted. "But how can you show him?" her partner asked. "I know how," the other assured her. "We will tell him that we will come again to continue our conversation."

They then told me, in Hebrew, what they had decided, but to their amazement, I responded in Russian, "I must share with you what is right because you are not right."

"Since you know Russian," the one said, "we must be honest with you. You are right—we have no power—but we won't give up."

"That's good," I said. "Don't give up. Pray to our Father in heaven and ask Him to reveal the truth to you."

—1975

## WHY HAVE WE LIVED
## SO LONG WITHOUT HIM?

Here in Israel, the people are very tired of war, as am I. Russian immigrants living here want to know how we can live in a country that has been so long without peace. "Don't you grow tired?" they asked. "Yes, I am tired of war," I replied, "but I have peace in my heart."

They wondered how this could be, when we don't know what tomorrow will bring. "How can we have peace in our hearts? It is impossible." I told them that it is possible. "But, if you want peace, you must first let the peace of God rule in your hearts." "How can this be?" they asked. "How can we know that God is in our hearts?" "Pray in His name, and you will see God change your life, as He did mine. You will receive blessing from above because it is written, 'without me ye can do nothing' (Jn. 15:5)."

They asked me how I came to know all of this, and I responded, "I came to believe through faith in the Lord Jesus.

It is a fact that without Him we cannot have peace in our hearts, in our homes, or in the streets with our friends." "How do you know this is true?" they questioned. "Did God speak to you?" "Yes," I answered, "through His Word. God is my Father, and when I pray to Him, I find rest and have great joy in my heart. If you have joy, you will also have peace."

The conversation continued, and I shared with them that the Lord has given me peace and great happiness. No one else can give these things except Him. I gave them each a Russian Bible and told them that everything they wanted to know could be found there. They were happy to receive the Bibles and promised to read them. I told them to first pray to the Lord for understanding, for without the Holy Spirit's guidance we cannot comprehend anything.

"Zvi," they asked, "are you a Christian?" "Yes," I replied. "I am a Hebrew-Christian." "Ah—now we know to whom we are speaking," they said. "How can you believe that Jesus is the Son of God? Is this possible? If so, can you prove it?" "Yes," I answered, "it is possible. In Genesis 1:26 God said, 'Let *us* make man in *our* image.' Jesus was a man. In Psalm 2:7 God said, 'Thou art my Son; this day have I begotten thee.' "

"These things are in our own Scriptures. Why have we lived so long without receiving Him as our Savior?" they asked. "That's a good question," I replied. "Many times Moses told God that His Chosen People were stiff-necked. But God, in His mercy, gave His only begotten Son to die for our sins and to rise again. Through Him we can receive forgiveness of our sins."

"But if we receive Jesus as our Savior, we will no longer be Jewish," they argued. "Look at me," I told them. "I believe in Jesus and yet I am still a Jew. In fact, I have served in the Israeli army since 1948 and have gone through all the difficult times. I am doing the very best I can for my country. I try to give my testimony to all those who have never heard about the Lord. It is only through Him that we can receive blessing."

These men were extremely interested in our conversation and in my faith in the Lord Jesus, which brought about such a change in my life. I feel that the Lord is speaking to them. It is my prayer that they will come to know Him as their Savior and Lord.

—1976

# HOW CAN I BELIEVE IN GOD?

People here in Israel are tense and extremely nervous. This is partly due to the economic situation. When I try to speak with them, many say, "There is no longer a God in the world because He sees and allows this nation, which He has chosen, to fall down. How can we believe in God?"

One man asked, "What do you think, Zvi?" I replied, "What you say is not true. God has chosen us and brought us to this Promised Land. We shall live and not die. If God wants us to die, He can certainly bring it about. In October 1973, when the Arab armies attacked us, the Israeli population was in a very demoralized condition. Why did God spare us? And why are we living now? We are still living and are still a nation because God loves us. He wants us to be His chosen nation, as He promised our fathers. Is it not true that we love our children? Of course we do. If we do not punish them for their misdeeds, they will continue to do as they wish. We do not punish our children because we hate them and desire to take revenge against them. No! No! And it is the same with our God.  He loves us intensely; therefore, He punishes us when we need it until the time comes when we ask His forgiveness. If people ask for forgiveness, change their ways, and turn to God, He will bless them.  If you do so, you and all your friends will know the truth about the Lord our God.  You see, He does not strike revenge upon us. And, when He makes a promise, He keeps it!  He is not as we humans are.  It is an easy thing to make a promise, but it is sometimes difficult to keep it."

After that, this man asked, "What do you think I should do? Should I believe in God, as you say?" "Yes," I replied.  "But why don't you ask God what to do, instead of asking me?"  With surprise he said, "How can I ask God?  Do you mean that He will answer me?  How can I speak with Him?"  I told him that he could go directly to God in prayer because He is our father, and He will answer him.  "What shall I say?  How shall I pray?" he questioned.

At this point, I opened the Bible and read for him the Lord's teaching about prayer.  I started to read from Matthew 6:9, "Our Father, who art in heaven...."  I also read from Matthew 5 what the Lord taught the large multitude that was on the mountain with Him.

Then this man realized whom I was speaking about.  "Jesus?" he said incredulously.  "He is not for the Jews.  He was against our Torah.  How can I believe in Him?"  I then read from Galatians 3:10:  "Cursed is everyone that continueth not in all things which are written in the book of the law, to do them."  This was another surprise to him, and he said, "Jesus is the great enemy of the Jews."

"That is what people say.  And you, my friend, believe them." He thought for a moment and then replied, "That is how I felt before, but not now."  Then we read together John 3:16:  "For God so loved the world, that he gave his only begotten Son, that whosoever believeth in him should not perish, but have everlasting life."

"This is all so new to me," he said.  "It would be nice if you would give me some books, so that I may read about these things for myself and share them with my friends. I want to show them how they lied to me. I will visit you every week, and you can teach me from the Bible."

Through this man, two other families came to me, and I gave them my testimony about the Lord. I was sure that after such a lengthy conversation about our Savior, they would not return, but the Lord opened their hearts and now they are our guests every week. I also visit in their homes, and we have become good friends. All of these dear people are now secret Christian believers. Perhaps one day soon they will openly acknowledge Jesus as their Messiah and Lord.

—1976

## HOW IS IT WITH YOUR SOUL?

This week my three older children—Ruth, Meno, and Victor—told me they were going to a hospital for old people and play their instruments for them. I had some free time that evening, so I accompanied them. I remembered the man who is in charge of the hospital, as I had a long discussion with him about a year ago. And so it was that I went with my children to this old folks home. The people were all about 80 years of age or older, and most were quite sick.

The first song my children played was from Psalm 121:5-8, which starts with the words, "The LORD is thy keeper." Then they played from Isaiah 60:1, "Arise, shine; for thy light is come, and the glory of the LORD is risen upon thee." The old people were very happy and sang along with the children. You see, every Jew knows these songs. The sad thing is that they do not know the one of whom the songs speak.

I was very surprised to see signs on the walls, written in large letters, stating, "Blessed is he that cometh in the name of the Lord." A year before, when I spoke with the doctor in charge of the hospital, he said, "Jews who believe in Jesus are not welcome in Israel." What had happened?

When my children finished, this doctor approached them and congratulated them on their fine playing. He asked them to come and play again and said that he would be happy to meet with their father. But when I came up to him, he seemed to be afraid. He said, "I know you, but I cannot remember from where." I said, "Yes, I remember you very well." He then became even more frightened. I asked, "What is the matter? Do you think I am a policeman? I am not. We were together in the Army for a short time last year." He then remembered me and the long discussion we had.

I pointed to the signs and asked what had caused the apparent shift in his attitude. He said, "Things have changed. We are living in different times." He then asked, "Are you the same? How have you been?" I replied, "Yes, I am the same believer. I am happy that the Lord is my Savior and that I can open my heart to Him in every situation." "I believe you," he said.

"If that is so," I asked, "why don't you open your heart to the Lord? Now you are a doctor, but there will come a time when you must give back to the Lord what He has given to you. The body is nothing, but how is it with your soul? If you do not put your trust in the Lord, you will be lost forever. You are not a child, you know. We are here talking now, but in an hour we both could be dead. Save your life! Believe in the Lord now!"

He said, "In this hospital, I am the boss. I am a big man. But, after what you have said to me, I can see that if I were to die now, I would be lost." I then gave him a Bible and said, "Read this and pray. Then, if you ask Him, God will come into your heart." He went on, "I am a very rich man, but I have no peace with myself." "I am much richer than you," I told him, "because I have the Lord in my heart. I am happy, and He gives me peace. You too can have this peace, but it is only available through His mercy."

He thanked me for the Bible and made me promise that my children would return. He said, "You are all welcome!"

—1976

## FOOD FOR THOUGHT

Recently I have been working near the Hebrew University in Jerusalem, and sometimes I have contact with the students there. They try to act very intelligent because they are studying at such a fine school. One day I told them, "You think you know everything, but you still have much to learn." They responded, "We know about great people, such as Shakespeare, Tolstoi, Einstein, Mozart, Brezniev, Kennedy, and others like them." I replied, "To you, these people may have been very great, but not to God—and not to me either. They were simply gifted men. If you were in a very desperate situation in life, perhaps close to death, would you call on Shakespeare and say, 'Shakespeare, save me'? Or would you say, 'Mozart, help me'? No! In times of trouble, people call on God. He is the one who gave Himself for us, and anyone who comes to Him in simple faith will be saved. He alone can give you everything you need in this life, and He alone can save your eternal soul."

"If this is so," they said, "and if God has given you so much, what can He give to us?" I replied, "God will give you peace in your hearts, happiness, hope, and, most important of all, He will give you everlasting forgiveness of your sins." "How do you know all of this?" they questioned. "Have you graduated from a school of theology?" "No," I answered, "but I know in my heart that the Lord has done these things for me, and He has given me the Holy Spirit, who keeps me and gives me the power to talk to you in this manner."

Then they said, "Of course, you must have read some books on this subject." "Oh, yes," I replied. "I have read a great deal, but mostly one book. This book is more important than the thousands of books you can read in your school. It is the Holy Bible, and it is greater than any of the books written by your great men because the Bible was written by men who were inspired by the Holy Spirit of God."

They wanted to know why I was telling them all of this, and I said, "Because I want you to be as I am, free from your sins. Then you won't think only of the things of this life, things that are without hope and that can cause you to hate your family, your friends, even yourselves—things that cause you to make many mistakes." "Don't you ever make mistakes?" they asked. "Yes, I do," I replied, "because I am no more perfect than you are. But when I make mistakes, I go to my heavenly Father and pray for His forgiveness. Then I go on from there, trying to do the best I can. Because I fear God, He protects me and keeps me from ways that are not pleasing to Him. I have the Holy Spirit within me, and He keeps me from deep sin, but you are not kept from sin, even though you are students at the great Hebrew University."

They told me that I would make a good lecturer and that I had given them much food for thought. They then asked how I had come to know so much about God. I told them, "There is only one way to know about God and His Son Jesus, and that is through the Bible." At this, one of them said, "I have read the Bible several times. Why don't I believe as you do?" "Because you have read it as a natural man," I told him. "If you all will read the Bible, asking God to speak to your hearts, you will receive what I now have—peace *from* Him and *with* Him."

I pray that these young people will have their eyes and hearts opened to God through the truths of His Word.

—1978

## THE LORD IS YOUR ATONEMENT

In Israel, the people are preparing for the feast of Rosh Hashanah—the New Year—followed by the greatest feast of all, Yom Kippur—the Day of Atonement, or, as it is called in Israel, the Day of Judgment. This is the only feast that the people really fear. Thirty days before the feast, they begin to pray, day after day and night after night, for forgiveness. This is the only time of year that they do this. After the Day of Atonement, prayer will be forgotten until next year.

Recently some people came to me and said, "We must talk to you again, and you know why. We want you to forget about your strange ways and come with us to pray." I asked who had sent them to me, and they replied, "No one sent us; we have come on our own." "No," I responded, "you did not come on your own, but I know who sent you. It was God!" They were shocked at this, but I continued, "Yes, God sent you so I could tell you that I don't have to go with you to pray for forgiveness. God has already forgiven my sins." "Oh yes," they agreed, "He forgives us every year at the time of the great feast." "That is not what I mean," I countered. "I came to God only one time. I gave my heart to Him and put my faith and trust in Him. At that time He forgave my sins, and I am sure of this. Now I don't have to fear the feast every year, as you do. If you will do the same thing, He will forgive your sins also, once forever. God has said, 'Abide in me, and I in you' [Jn. 15:4]."

They were not interested in anything I said and went on, "We promise that if you will do as we ask, you will have no more trouble with us." I responded, "I do not live in fear, and I am especially not afraid of you. I fear only God." "How can you fear God when you do not believe in Him, but in Jesus?" they asked. "I will be glad to answer that question," I said, "and then you will know that all of the offerings you make at the time of the feast are in vain. They are nothingness. The Lord said, 'I am full of the burnt offerings of rams' [Isa. 1:11]. I believe in only one offering, and that is the offering of the Lord Himself, who gave Himself for us."

"From what book did you take that?" they asked. Quickly I opened the Bible to the Book of Isaiah and read chapter 53. Then I told them, "Here you have my answer. He is the one to whom I have given my heart and my trust, and He has given me peace and assurance. I know that when my time comes to leave this world, I will dwell in the house of the Lord forever. Now you have come to tell me that I may experience more trouble from you. Well, I have had so many troubles in the past that I am not afraid anymore." "Not even about your life?" they demanded. "No," I answered, "because I know to whom I belong."

At this point they said, "If you are not afraid of us, then let us make a cease-fire and speak together as good friends." "That is what I have been waiting for," I replied. "I want you to know that I do not hate you. In fact, I would like to be able to speak with you as a friend—not because I fear you but because I love you. It is written that we are to love our enemies. You are my dear friends, and you are welcome to visit me anytime you wish." They said, "We cannot believe this!"

Then my children played their instruments for these people, and they shared a meal with my family. I could feel the Spirit of the Lord working, and after we had eaten I asked how they felt. "Very good," they replied. "If that is so," I continued, "may I read to you some things from the New Testament and tell you why I am so happy?" They agreed, and I began to read Romans 12, particularly verses 9-21.

When I finished reading, one man said, "These things are nice to hear, but I have a question. You said that Jesus loved His enemies?" "Yes," I replied. "If that is so, then why did the Germans, who are Christians, persecute the Jewish people so badly?"

I replied, "I am sure that they were not true believers in the Lord. It was only a confederation in His name, until the persecution was over. You all know what has happened in Germany since then. Many of the people are again calling on the Lord, and they are sorry for what they did. Of course, they are not really clean within. They are only hoping that they are clean, just as you hope when you pray and sacrifice for the great feast. When I received the Lord as my Savior, I was done with vain prayers and sacrifices. I received His love, His grace, His mercy. On the Day of Atonement, you will go to the synagogue and pray and cry, but you will not be sure if the Lord has forgiven your sins. I am sure! He has given me complete confidence of this.

"My friends, why do you continue to live in fear? The Lord is your atonement. He will receive you into His family, as He has received me, and He will forgive your sins. You too can be done with the offering of rams. You all know very well that you came here through hate. You came to warn me, but what has happened? The love of the Lord has been with us as we have talked in this place. If the Lord of Hosts had not left a few survivors for His name, we would have become as Sodom and Gomorrah. We should thank the Lord that He is with us."

These people left my home, but not as they had come. They left with love in their hearts and happy smiles on their faces. Praise the Lord!

—1979

## THE LORD WILL NEVER REJECT YOU

People are never sure of themselves. They say something today, but tomorrow they change their minds. Some people are sorry for this fault, and that is good. But others see only the dark side of things, and they will not turn from their ways.

Near me lives a happy couple—she about 60 years old and he about 62. I have visited them from time to time, and the husband always wants to talk about world problems. On a recent visit, I tried to speak about the Bible, but he said, "Please, the Bible is very far from me, and I don't like to speak about it." I told him, "You must realize that you are no longer a child. Today you are here, but tomorrow you may lose your life. I do not mean only the body, which is nothing, but you may also lose the most important thing, your soul."

The wife was always much different. She had gladly received a Bible from me and was very interested in knowing about eternal life. I read to her Psalm 23, ending with, "I will dwell in the house of the LORD forever." The husband asked, "Do you want to die now just to receive this everlasting life?" I replied, "Everything comes in its own time. It is written in the Bible, 'The LORD gave, and the LORD hath taken away; blessed be the name of the LORD' [Job 1:21]. When my time comes to die, I will not be sorry because I know in whom I have put my trust."

He then said to his wife, "Do you see how crazy he is? He puts his trust in the Bible." "Oh no," I responded. "I don't put my trust in the Bible but in God." This statement made him very unhappy, and he took the Bible that I had given to his wife and cast it out the window. Then he said, "Now your faith is out!" "No," I replied, "I have my faith with me in my heart. You can cast away many Bibles, but you can do nothing against me. You are really fighting against yourself. Your wife has received the Lord, and she will have eternal life. I believe with all my heart that, even after all you have done, the Lord will forgive you too. The way is always open." He then began to shout, "What? Go! Go away from here! Who are you to speak about my future? My wife will not receive your Bible or your faith. Never! Never!"

His wife quietly said to me, "I do believe, and I know that I have everlasting life." Before I left I told her, "You don't have to believe these things just because I said them. You have a free choice. But if you will pray to our Father in heaven, He will show you the right way. He will show you what to do." She replied, "Thank you, and I will do that. I am sorry that my husband doesn't want to believe this also." I replied, "It is written, 'the just shall live by his faith' [Hab. 2:4]."

And so I left the home, but not before the husband told me, "I don't ever want to see you here again! Not ever!" I was not surprised at this because it was not the first time he had spoken like that to me. On my way home, I prayed for him, and I gave thanks to the Lord for his wife, who had received Him.

Several days after that visit, I received a telephone call from this man who had sent me away from his home. He said, "Please come to me quickly. My wife died two days ago. I am sure that she is at home, but I must see you." This was a distress signal, so I immediately left everything and went to his home. "I'm here," I said as I arrived. "Oh, my dear man, I love you; please forgive me," he cried. "Believe me, I have nothing against you. That is all in the past. I am alone in this world now. What can I do? Who will be with me now?"

I answered, "There is only one person who can help you." "Who?" he asked. "The Lord, our Savior," I replied. "If you put your trust in Him, as your wife did, you will no longer be alone." He replied, "I cannot believe because I cast away the Holy Bible." I assured him, "The Lord is a God of love. He will never reject you. You can see it here in the Bible, which before was so far from you." I then read Jeremiah 31:31-35, so that he would know that all people have the opportunity to go to heaven if they give their hearts to the Lord.

He talked to me as a small child and was very hungry to hear God's Word. He wanted to know more and more about Him, and time was not important. No one had come to comfort him after his wife's death, and he was bitter. He continued, "Please help me; I am so alone. You can come to my home whenever you like." I told him, "If you receive the Lord, you will never be alone. You can speak with Him at anytime, as with a best friend—even as with a father. What more could you want? The Lord has said, 'Fear not; for I am with thee' [Isa. 43:5]."

He begged, "Please come to see me everyday. You are welcome. I promise that I will never do what I did before." "If you promise this to God," I told him, "He will forgive you." He was very sorry for what he had done, but I told him, "All is forgiven and forgotten. Now, I beg you, open up a new life for yourself, a life full of light." He gladly received what I told him.

—1979

## FAITH BY THE SWORD—
## OR FAITH BY LOVE?

Israel is a small country, and at times we feel as if we are sheep among wolves. But even though we are small, we remain strong because the Lord is with us.

Most people living in Israel, both Jews and Arabs, do not know the Lord. The Arabs especially are far from knowing about His love. But we believers are God's witnesses, and now is the time to tell them of that love.

There is a saying, "If Mohammed won't come to the mountain, the mountain will come to Mohammed." It is like that with us, but it is difficult to go to an Arab village and preach the Word of God.

One day some of my Arab neighbors came to my home extremely upset, saying, "How can we receive Bibles when they include the New Testament?" They were very confused, so I said, "Before you receive the Bible, I will explain it to you, if you wish." They agreed and appreciated my help. I then opened my New Testament and told them how to put their faith in the Lord Jesus. The mention of that name surprised them, and they asked, "How can you speak about Jesus? You are a Jew."

So began a long discussion about faith in the Lord Jesus and the difference between faith by the sword and faith by love. I told these Arabs, "Your faith comes by the sword, and those who do not believe as you do are killed. God has given freedom to every creature. He has said, 'I have loved thee with an everlasting love' [Jer. 31:3]." One Arab remarked, "God said that only to the people of Israel." I quickly turned to John 3:16 to prove that God's love is available to all nations, including the Arabs. "It is written, 'Thou shalt love thy neighbor as thyself' [Mk. 12:31]. It does not say, 'Love the Jew, or the American, but not the Arab.' Loving your neighbor means loving your enemy as well."

Then they wanted to know how I came to believe on the Lord, since I am a Jew. "How can this be possible?" they asked. I replied, "Our faith does not come from any propaganda literature or by force, but by God's mercy and love. What the Lord did for us, He did because of His love. You, as Arabs, came to me, a Jew, and I received you as best friends, even though I know that you hate me with all your hearts. But the Lord said that we are to love those who hate us and pray for them because love is of God."

Still not understanding what I meant, they asked, "Why do you serve in the army if you love your enemies." I answered, "I serve because I am a citizen of Israel. Even Jesus said, 'Render...unto Caesar the things which are Caesar's; and unto God, the things that are God's' [Mt. 22:21]."

I then related an incident that occurred during the Six-Day War. I went to the home of a wealthy Arab family and found gold and diamonds worth millions of dollars. The owners were afraid that I would take their possessions, but I quieted them, assuring them, "All I am looking for is guns and ammunition. But if a soldier who was not a believer had come to search your home, your possessions

THE BEST OF ZVI

would have been taken." As I finished my story, I explained to my guests, "This is the big difference between people who believe in Jesus and people who do not. And, it does not matter if they are Jews, Arabs, or any other nationality on the face of the earth."

It was hard for them to believe my story, so I offered to call a taxi and take them to the home of this Arab family, so that they could ask them about it themselves. But they finally accepted the fact that even war can't break our love for our enemy because the love of our Savior is in us.

Please pray for these Arab neighbors and for the thousands of other Arabs in Israel, that they will be reached with the gospel of the Lord Jesus Christ.

—1979

## HOW CAN YOU BE SO HAPPY?

A new law was recently passed in Israel saying that *Hebrew-Christians* are now to be referred to simply as *Christians*. So was the decision of the courts, and it cannot be changed. The subject is closed!

After this law went into effect, I received many reactions from some of my so-called *friends*. Some *congratulated* me saying, "You must be happy now that you are no longer a Jew, but only a Christian." Others asked, "What are you doing in Israel? You are not a Jew now, but a Christian."

I told them all the same thing. "I was born a Jew and am living in the Promised Land. But, I did not become a *good* Jew until I received the Lord Jesus as my Savior. Now I feel that I am a better Jew than you. You call yourselves Jews, but nothing more. As you live, so you will die. It is not enough to call yourself a Jew. You must follow in His steps." "In whose steps?" they asked, and I replied, "In the steps of the Lord. You cannot be just a Jew, or an Arab, or one from any other country. Everyone has the privilege of worshiping the Lord, and with Him there is no difference. The Lord does not ask who you are or to which nation you belong. He is the Father of all nations, the Father of the world. He will receive all who come to Him, and He treats everyone the same. He does not say, 'This one is a Jew, and this one is a Christian. This one is rich, and this one is poor.' All those who belong to Him belong to one family—the family of God."

Some of them remarked, "Zvi, you say that once you believe, you cannot turn away from it. Why is that?" I asked in return, "Are you more happy than I or my children? What more do you have than I have? How can I turn away from everything that is mine?" "And what is that?" they asked. I replied, "I have a great property waiting for me in heaven. Oh, I know that you have more earthly property than I have, but you also have more cares."

When I said this, one man asked, "Who told you that? Are you saying that you are happier than I am?" "Yes," I replied. "If that is so," he said, "I want to see it with my own eyes, and I also want to show you what I have!" Although he looked very sad, he didn't understand how I could be happier than he with all of his property and possessions, so he invited me to his home.

He did have a very large house, and very nice, but happiness is more important than the size of a house. He has two sons, and from the expressions on their faces, you would think they were poor. They looked sick and bitter. There were no smiles on their faces, and, in fact, they looked as if they were in mourning. I was almost afraid to speak to this man, I felt so sorry for him. He had shown me a nice house, but nothing more. It all seemed so empty.

He finally asked, "What do you think of my house?" "It is nice," I replied, "but you are very poor." "What?" he exclaimed, as if he could not believe his ears. "How can you say that? Look at my large house, my fine furniture, and all the other fine things I have." "But it is not enough," I told him. "Why?" he asked, and I replied,

"Because you have no happiness in your home. Therefore, you really have nothing at all." "Do you think you have more than me?" he demanded. "Oh yes," I said, "because I have the Lord in my heart, and in Him I have great possessions." "You speak like a crazy man!" he said. I then asked, "Do you have time to come to my home? Of course, I do not have such nice furniture and other things, as you have, but I have something in my home that you do not have. You see, the light of the Lord is there."

He and his two sons then accompanied me to my home. When we arrived, my youngest son was arguing with one of his brothers, but after a short time that was over, and the children gladly played music and sang for our guests. Then my wife Naomi provided some fine hospitality for them, which she does so well. There was happiness such as this man had never known, yet he seemed saddened by it. He remarked, "Now I see what you mean, but how can you be so happy?" "Because it is written, 'whoso trusteth in the LORD, happy is he' [Prov. 16:20). You can share in our happiness." "Oh yes, I want that," he said, "but how can I do it? We are Jewish and you are Christians." I told him, "Who we are makes no difference. The important thing is that we have one God and one law. You can read the Holy Bible for yourself and learn of the one about whom it is written."

By this time, his boys said that they wanted to stay with us, and the father could see how happy they were, even though our home contained no great treasures, such as they had. They were thrilled when my children asked them to go outside and play with a simple ball. The man appeared sad again and did not know what to say. After some time he confided, "I am ashamed to say this, but I am jealous of you."

I told him, "You can now see that you are a rich man, but nothing more." He replied, "Yes, I now know that I am very poor, and you are much richer than I. I am ready to give everything and anything to be as happy as you." "And you can be so, right this very minute," I told him. "Such happiness can be yours, and you can tell your children and family that you have put your trust in the Lord. He will do what must be done in your life. Of this I am sure. It is written, 'come, take up the cross, and follow me' [Mk. 10:21]. It is easy to see that everyone who chooses to follow Him is happy, not bitter as you and the others like you, who have no faith in the Lord." "How did you come to believe in Him?" he asked. He seemed very interested, so I was delighted to share my testimony with him.

Then he said, "You are very happy, and I want to be that way also, but I do not have the courage to do it." "Of course you have," I told him. "Just open your heart to Him, as to a Father. I will leave you alone for a while to think on these things." I then went outside to play with the children, and when we came back inside, he was smiling. The light had come to him and had given him true happiness.

—1979

## YOU HAVE NEVER SEEN THE LIGHT

On my way home from work recently, for some *unknown* reason I went by a different route than I usually take. As I was walking along, I wondered why I was there; how did this happen? But, I received the answer in the end.

It was a very warm day, and I went home through the Mea-Shearim quarter of Jerusalem. That is where the extremely religious people live—people who have never left that small area in their entire lives because they were warned when they were children that the people who live outside Mea-Shearim are atheists. Of course, that is not true, and, as you walk through the streets, it is easy to see that even the residents there do not believe it. That day I could not believe my eyes when I saw three young men, who belong to one of the most fanatic groups, gambling for money on the street.

I had to know what was happening, so I took courage and asked them, "Am I dreaming, or is it true what my eyes see?" The three looked at me with surprise and asked, "Why do you think you are dreaming?" I answered, "Because I see here the same thing that goes on in the 'free world' outside of Mea-Shearim. Today it is a lottery; I suppose tomorrow it will be card playing. This is a shock to me." "Why?" they asked, and I replied, "Because it is written in the Bible, 'Ye cannot serve God and money' [Mt. 6:24]. I also see that you are fighting each other with all your hearts while you are gambling, and this is against the will of God. No one should know these things better than you. I am sure you realize that what you are doing is against the Lord."

They said, "Now you have gone too far. Tell us who you are, that you think you can tell us what to do. Look at yourself and look at us. We have our heads covered, but you are doing as the *goyim* [*Gentiles*] do, having your head uncovered." I asked, "Is that all I am doing wrong? If so, I can see that you are blind?" "Why?" they demanded. "Because you think that all you must do to please God is cover your heads." "Do you want us to go around with our heads uncovered like you?" they asked. I replied, "I cannot give you orders, but I can make a proposal." "Let's hear it," they said.

"First," I told them, "you must truly want to follow the Lord. Then, don't gamble because it is against His will and will not give you any success, only troubles. Also, you must stop making the mistake of thinking that covering your heads will please God. The important thing is to have your hearts covered with flesh and not stone."

At this they said, "You speak like an angel, but tell us who you really are." This is a question I hear almost every day, so I was not surprised. I told them, "I am a Jew who is saved, and I believe in the living God." They responded, "Now you think you have to come here and tell us how to live? Well, you can believe that we have enough teachers right here—maybe too many." I then said, "The sad thing is that with all your teachers, you are going deeper and deeper into sin, and there is no one to tell you the truth about the Lord and how to be saved." "Do you mean that our rabbis are wrong?" they asked. I answered, "Your rabbis also need help from above, just as we all do. They are not special people; they are mere mortals. Even though you have been trained by these highly educated men, I can see that you are poor in knowledge, and the rabbis are poorer than you."

They then began to attack me with many curses, but the Lord has told us, "bless them that curse you…pray for them who despitefully use you, and persecute you" (Mt. 5:44). As they were shouting at me, a man with a long white beard, about 65 years of age, passed by the kiosk where we were talking. He was a rabbi, so I stopped him and asked, "Do you see what your pupils are doing?" "They are not my pupils," he replied, "they are only an imitation." I could see that he was ashamed because of these three young men, and he said, "I am very tired; I must sit down." He took a seat at one of the tables and invited me to sit with him, even though the three were still shouting at me.

I brought a soft drink to him, and it was now just the two of us speaking together. The rabbi said, "Tell me who you are." You can see how many times I must answer that question, but this time it was special. His question came from his heart, and I felt that he was very thirsty—not for water but for knowledge. He looked at me intently, waiting for an answer. I thought again of where I was—in the very headquarters of the most fanatic ones in Israel—and the three young men were still there, waiting to "eat me up" without salt because of their hatred for me.

Although I was a bit nervous at the beginning, I received great courage from the Lord and said to this nice gentleman, "I am only a man, but I believe in the living God." "I do also," he said. I responded, "But I have been born again." "What!" he exclaimed. "How can this be? You are no longer a child, and you cannot possibly mean that you were dead and are now alive again."

I told him, "I know this is going to be a great surprise to you, but, yes, I was dead in sin, and now I have been saved from my sins and am alive because I am born again in the Spirit." That was something completely new to him, and he thought I was crazy at first, but in time he realized what I meant and he became frightened. His whole body started to tremble, even though it was a very warm day. I asked, "Are you feeling ill?" "I was feeling well," he replied, "but now I don't know what is wrong with me. This is the first time I have ever trembled so, and I want to know why." I told him, "It could be that this is the beginning for you and that soon you too will become born again. Perhaps you are only waiting for an order from above."

He then leaned close to me and said, "Please speak quietly because, as you know, even the walls have ears in this place." In my heart, I wanted everyone around us to hear the conversation, but I realized that, while this man was afraid, he was very thirsty for the Word of God, so I spoke softly.

After a while the rabbi said, "I am no longer trembling and I feel fine again. Now I can open my mouth and speak. I was born in Mea-Shearim, and now I am past 60 years old. Believe me, I know every stone in this place because I have never left this area in my whole life. My grandfathers came to Jerusalem from Tiberias and Safed, in the north of Israel. I am the seventh generation of my family to be born in Israel, and I was educated here in Jerusalem."

I told him, "I am sorry that you have lived all your life in such darkness. You have never seen the light." "Oh, you are mistaken," he said. "We have night and day here. Of course it is dark at night, but during the day we have light." "No, my friend," I responded, "here in Mea-Shearim you have darkness always—never any light. Since you are a rabbi, you may think it is wrong of me to say such things, but if you want to hear more, I will gladly continue." "Please tell me more," he said.

"Even though a man has a great education, without God in his heart he is walking in darkness. Even when the sun shines brightly, he cannot see the true light. He only knows everlasting darkness, and especially here in Mea-Shearim. You can see with your own eyes the picture before you. Today they are gambling, tomorrow it will be card playing, and after that—well, who knows?" "What can we do to stop this?" he asked. I replied, "One way is to be an obedient child of God by trusting the Messiah Jesus and following Him in the waters of baptism." "What!" he said. "Never! Never! This is what the *meshumeds* [*traitors*] do. It is impossible to receive the Holy Spirit only by coming to the waters of baptism." "No, that is not what you must do to become born again," I corrected him. "You must first give your heart to the Lord. The water will not wash away your sins. Baptism is a sign that you have received Jesus as your Savior."

Although we were having an open conversation, I could tell that he did not want to hear about the Holy Spirit, so I said, "I want to give you facts to back up what I say. Would you like to hear what our prophets have written about the Holy Spirit?" "Yes," he replied, asking, "Do you have the Holy Scriptures with you?" I gladly took out my small Hebrew Bible and read Ezekiel 36:25-27.

After this he asked, "How do you know these things?" "Because I am walking in the light," I replied. "Even at night, when it is dark, the Lord is my light and in Him is no darkness." "All of this is good," he told me, "but you must realize that I was born here and have lived my whole life here. Do you want me to leave this place now? Where would I go?" I responded, "How long will you continue in darkness? Is it not enough that you and your pupils have not come to the light? Do you want the future generations to live in darkness also? They will be born in sin and die in sin, and no will come and say to them, 'Enough! No more darkness!' As it is written, 'Arise, shine; for thy light is come' [Isa. 60:1].

Someone must tell the people this. You did not know these things, but I have told you, and now you must go and tell your pupils. If this is too hard for you, I will be glad to come with you. Surely you remember that Moses went to Pharaoh, even though he was afraid, because the Lord promised to go with him."

I could see that he was very close to crying. He was so friendly toward me and wanted to hear more and more. He said, "This is the first lesson I have ever received in Mea-Shearim that has gone so deep into my heart." Then I pleaded, "My dear friend, leave all this darkness behind you and let us walk together in the light of the Lord Jesus, who died for you."

It was interesting to see that the three young men never stopped fighting among themselves while I talked with the rabbi, although it is possible that they heard our conversation. I wanted to try and stop them, but the rabbi said, "Let them fight. What the eye does not see, the heart does not grieve for." "No, my friend," I responded, "that is not the way the Lord wants it. If you become born again, they will also fight against you. You know that when we first began to talk, you were also against me, but now we are good friends. I have learned the hard way that it is easy to make enemies but difficult to make friends."

I then went over to the three and said, "Please stop your fighting. You must be tired of it by now. Come on over and have a soft drink with me." They accepted, and I bought drinks for all of them, including another one for the rabbi. Then they forgot about their fighting and asked again, "Who are you?" When the rabbi heard this, he said, "I must go now. I am afraid." As he was leaving, I said, "Remember, no more darkness," to which he replied, "Only light." Then I turned my attention to the three young men and told them what they wanted to know—who I am and what I believe—and this time they listened.

I thank the Lord that He was with me that day, directing my path to that place and giving me the words to say. I pray that this dear old rabbi and the three young men will have their eyes opened and come to know Him, the one who is the true Light of the world.

—1981

## WE CAN FORGET ALL OF THAT
## BECAUSE OF THE LORD

We often say that no ill is without its good, but until the good news comes, we must usually go through many troubles. Even the worst people have some good in them, and I would like to tell you about one such person.

Early last year, many of my co-workers seemed interested in knowing about the Lord. They all knew that I was a believer, and so they felt that I could tell them about Him. Of course, I was happy to speak about Him to these people, who had always thought of Jesus as someone who died and no longer existed. Even though they felt that way, there was something about Him that would not let them rest. They wanted to know who He was and why, such a long time after His death, He was still remembered. They felt there must be some secret involved, and they wanted to know what it was.

I told them, "There is nothing secret about the Lord. You can see what is written about Him in black and white in the Bible. But, I am at your service; you can ask me whatever you like." I have found that the question and answer method is a good system. I am not a Bible teacher, but through His Holy Spirit, my walk with Him, and His great love for me, everything is possible. The right answers always seem to come at the right times, and because He was present in our discussions, everything went well with my co-workers.

Then one day a new worker joined us—a man full of hatred, blindness, and jealousy. It seemed that all of the evil present in the world could be found in this man. The first time he heard my friends ask me something about the Lord, he was shocked and asked, "How can you be friendly with this man, a believer? No! No! This is impossible." From that time on, it was as if the Devil had begun his act against me through this man. He unleashed a great storm against me. Even though he didn't know me, he did know that I was a believer, and that was enough for him. He did not need to know anything else. There was no milk or honey in his tongue; instead, he had a tongue of fire because the Devil was using him to create much hatred among the workers, and all of it directed at me. However, I was not afraid, and I prayed to my Savior that all of these men might truly come to know Him, have their sins forgiven, and be saved.

This evil continued for a long time, and there was no good news to be had. But, the Lord knew all about it, and the situation was in His hands. Finally, after all the hatred this man had stirred up against me, I was told that I must leave my job in five days.

But, what happened in the meantime? That night, the man who had caused me so much trouble was taken to the hospital and had to have emergency surgery. The next day, his wife came to the job site and asked if any of his "work friends" would give blood for him, as he needed two pints after the surgery. When she asked this, it seemed as if all of the men became deaf. Then I said, "I will give him a pint of blood, but he must know that it came from a believer—a Jewish believer whose Savior is the Lord Jesus Christ."

The other men exclaimed, "What? After all that he has done to you, are you now going to give him your blood? No! This is the time to take revenge!" I told them, "Now you can see the difference between me, a believer, and yourselves, who say you believe in God but call for revenge. At a time like this, he must be saved, both bodily and, what's more important, spiritually." They all became very quiet, and I went with the man's wife to the hospital and gave a pint of blood. Then, five days later, I left my job because of him.

Recently, after about a year had passed, one evening there was a knock at my door. When I opened it, there was a big surprise waiting for me. Who was standing there but this man, who had spoken with such fire against me, along with his wife and their two small children. Even more shocking than his presence was the fact that he apologized to me, saying, "I have had no rest all year, since the time that you had to leave work because of my blindness. I asked many people where you lived, but they would not give me your address because they were ashamed of what I had done against you and how they had hated you because of me. I cannot excuse myself, and I am even prepared to be cast away from your home tonight, and, of course, you would be right in doing so."

I told him, "No, I would not do that. The Lord has taught us to love our enemies." I then opened the New Testament, which this man hated so intensely, and read to him and his family Matthew 5:44: "Love your enemies, bless them that curse you, do good to them that hate you, and pray for them who despitefully use you, and persecute you." I then read Romans 12:17 and 19: "Recompense to no man evil for evil...for it is written, Vengeance is mine; I will repay, saith the Lord." Finally, I read a very important verse, Romans 12:20: "if thine enemy hunger, feed him; if he thirst, give him drink."

After this, with tears on his face, he asked himself, "Can this be true, after I was so bad to him?" His wife said, "Yes, you were bad;

you were more like a monster than a man, to have done the things you did." I then told them, "We can forget all of that because of the Lord. He is the one who died for us, and through Him we can receive forgiveness of our sins, as it is written in John 3:16, 'For God so loved the world, that he gave his only begotten Son, that whosoever believeth in him should not perish, but have everlasting life.' Then you can be happy in His salvation."

After I said this, I couldn't believe my eyes. What I saw was a man who before had no conscience, faith, or humanity, but now, because of what the Lord had done in him, he was as soft as butter in the summer. He asked, "What can I do for you?" "Nothing," I replied. "What you must do is for yourself. Pray to the Lord, our Savior. He can give you that which no one else can give. You must remember that when you were in the hospital, what I did for you was done through His love." He again wept and was very sorry.

—1981

# NO DREAMS—JUST FACTS

Sometimes we see things that are hard to believe, but we know they are so. It is also funny to see how grown people can be like children, and speak like them. They can confuse folklore and Bible truths.

Recently I was in the army again. One night we were on watch, and, of course, we were not allowed to sleep. The nights are very long when there is nothing to do. We must watch all night, and every hour seems like a year. One night I was on watch with some religious Jews who had many stories to tell, and so the hours slipped by quickly.

The first story was about a 90-year-old man who was blind from birth. In a dream, an angel asked why he did not read the Psalms. The blind man told the angel that he could not read because he could not see. When the angel asked him what he wanted, of course the blind man requested sight so that he could read the Psalms.

One by one, each soldier told his story. When they had all finished, they looked at me and asked, "Have you anything to say?" Sometimes it is difficult to begin with such people, but when they asked me, I knew that this was a special opportunity for the Lord.

I told them that all their stories were just dreams. "What I will now read for you is not a dream; it is real," I said. "It is about people who were blind, but then they received sight, and they followed the one who gave them that sight." "Where is this written?" they demanded. I opened my small Bible and read from Matthew 20:29-34 about the two blind men who cried out, "Have mercy on us, O Lord, thou Son of David" (v. 30). And, of course, the Lord is full of mercy, so He caused them to see. "This was not a dream," I told them. I then read Acts 3:6, where Peter said to the lame man, "Silver and gold have I none, but, such as I have, give I thee. In the name of Jesus Christ of Nazareth, rise up and walk." The lame man arose and walked.

When I finished, they said, "You have gone too far. How can you say the name of Jesus in our presence? You speak about Him as if He were holy!" "Of course He is holy," I replied, "and He always will be. He is everlasting." "If you continue to speak of Him, you will have trouble from us," they warned. "I am not afraid, not of you," I replied. "You are afraid of the truth, and so you speak of dreams and make them seem like facts. When I read for you from the Holy Scriptures, you all trembled with fear. The things I have told you are not dreams but facts."

"Why is it that you do not believe what our rabbis have written?" they asked. "Because they are all stories that they dreamed at night and wrote the next day," I replied. "How do you know this?" they asked. I said, "I know that I believe in one God, and what is written in His Bible is holy because it was written through His Holy Spirit and not by people who took their stories from dreams. Now you want me to believe the rabbis' stories as fact. Show me even one small point that is written about them in the Bible."

"Ha, ha! Now we can say we are equal," they said, "because there is nothing written about Jesus in the Bible either!" Again they gave me a good opportunity to speak about the Lord Jesus, so I started by reading Proverbs 30:4: "Who hath ascended up into heaven, or descended? Who hath gathered the wind in his fists? Who hath bound the waters in a garment? Who hath established all the ends of the earth? What is his name, and what is his son's name, if thou canst tell?" Then I read Daniel 3:25: "Lo, I see four men loose, walking in the midst of the fire, and they have no hurt; and the form of the fourth is like a son of the gods."

This was all new to these soldiers. They had for so long gone about in darkness, but now they were beginning to see the light— not a dream, but the truth.

After that they did not ask for any more stories. Instead, they wanted everyone to read a verse from the Bible and then discuss the verse. So, everyone took his turn. When it was my turn, I chose Isaiah 9:6: "For unto us a child is born, unto us a son is given, and the government shall be upon his shoulder; and his name shall be called Wonderful, Counselor, The Mighty God, The Everlasting Father, The Prince of Peace." Of course, I took the opportunity to illustrate the verse. Their eyes began to see, and their ears began to hear. I believe even their hearts began to open to the truth. I say this because earlier, when I read Scripture, they trembled with fear. Now they not only had no fear, but they took my Bible, which included the New Testament, and began to read it. They even asked for Bibles of their own containing the New Testament.

I read Isaiah 9:2: "The people that walked in darkness have seen a great light; they that dwell in the land of the shadow of death, upon them hath the light shined."

I thank the Lord that He can use every situation to bring glory to Himself. Out of their stories came my opportunity to testify for the Lord. He is in every place, and He can accomplish that which is impossible for us.

I pray for these soldiers as they have been confronted with the truth.

—1982

# NOT THIS TIME!

Two of my sons and my daughter are not at home these days. They have gone to the north—the Lebanese front—with the army. And now I have received a letter stating that the army wants me also, but I said, "Not this time!" I went to see the military officials and informed them that if they want me, they will also have to take my wife and my youngest son. I reminded them that I am now 53 years old and took an active part in the most dangerous duty in all four of Israel's previous wars. Then one of the officers said, "But you know how serious the situation is in the north, and we need everyone." I replied, "Yes, I know that, and I have given you my daughter and two of my sons. If you must have me, I repeat, then you must take my wife and my youngest son, and then all of our family will be in the army."

The officer said, "Wait a minute" and walked away. In a short time he returned with a solution. "You may stay at home for now, but we may have to call you if we need you, so be ready." "I am always ready," I said. He asked, "What do you mean?" and I responded, "I am ready to preach the good news of God to all those who want to hear about Him." "But you are not a rabbi, and I know that you are far from the teachings of the yeshiva [religious school]." "You are right," I told him, "but tell me, did Israel's Old Testament prophets go to a yeshiva or to great universities? No! When the Lord spoke to Moses the first time, did He ask him what type of education he had or how many doctorates he had received. He simply asked Moses to go and do His will, and Moses did, even though he was slow of speech. It was not Moses speaking, but God Himself who put the words in Moses' mouth. And that's how it is with me."

"What do you want to speak about?" the officer asked. I replied, "I want to tell you about the most important need of our time, or of any time—salvation." "But we are close to victory in the north," he said. "No, my friend, we are not," I responded. "There is another way, and it is 'Not by might, nor by power, but by my Spirit, saith the LORD of hosts' [Zech. 4:6]. The Lord has fought for us in the past, and He is doing so again."

"Who do you think is fighting for us in places like Tyre and Sidon?" he asked. "I can answer that," I said, "and not from any of your official papers but from the prophets of old. Jeremiah 47:4 tells us what the Lord is doing for us: 'Because of the day that cometh to spoil all the Philistines, and to cut off from Tyre and Sidon every helper that remaineth; for the LORD will spoil the Philistines, the remnant.' You can read about this war in many other places in the Bible, such as Ezekiel 26:3-4: 'Therefore, thus saith the Lord GOD: Behold, I am against thee, O Tyre, and will cause many nations to come up against thee, as the sea causeth its waves to come up. And they shall destroy the walls of Tyre, and break down her towers; I will also scrape her dust from her, and make her like the top of a rock.'

"The Lord has given us these passages to let us know what will take place, so that it will not be a surprise to us. This is only the beginning for this nation, and I am not speaking like other people who have no one serving in the north.  Even though my children are there, I can be at rest and have peace because I put my trust in the Lord.  Not many parents have more children in the north than I do, and since they have been gone I have received only one telephone call, but I am trusting in the Lord, whose promises are everlasting.  I even know who our enemies are."  "And just who are they?" he asked.  I replied, "You will find the answer in Isaiah 10:24: 'O my people that dwell in Zion, be not afraid of the Assyrian; he shall smite thee with a rod, and shall lift up his staff against thee.' Why should we be afraid?  We can be sure of His victory, and we do not have to worry about gaining the victory ourselves."

Then the officer asked, "Where do you get your confidence?"  I said, "I can answer that easily: 'Behold, God is my salvation; I will trust, and not be afraid' [Isa. 12:2].  If you are afraid, do as I did. Believe in the Son of God, and He will deliver you.  And, I am not alone; there are many people in Israel who believe this way.  Now is the time for the people of Israel to open their eyes to God's miracles on our behalf. There is no one in this nation who does not know the song taken from Joel 3:20, 'Judah shall dwell forever, and Jerusalem from generation to generation.' "

He then asked again, "How can you be so confident, especially when your children are in danger far away from home?"  I could not pass up such an opportunity, and we began a long conversation about faith in the Lord.  Finally he said, "If you think we don't know who you are, you are mistaken.  We know all about you, but we never knew that you and others like you were so bound to this land of ours."  I told him, "You must understand that we believe in the same heavenly Father, we read the same Bible, and we are loyal citizens of Israel, just as you are.  Why should we not love our country, and especially in time of trouble?  Now is the time for us to show that we are true friends of Israel and its citizens.  I have given my three children to fight for this land, and there is even more that I can give for my country." "What is that?" he asked.

I replied, "As I told you before, you can take me if you must. However, this time is different from the other wars, when all of my children were young. In 1948, 1956, 1967, and 1973, I took an active part, but this time my children have taken my place. I do not want to go and leave my wife and young son alone." "We know that you have been a good soldier," he said, "but you must realize that if this turns into a big war, you must go. We do not have as many people as our enemies." "That is true," I agreed, "but it is at times like this that you must trust in the Lord and remember what He said in Deuteronomy 7:17: 'If thou shalt say in thine heart, These nations are more than I; how can I dispossess them?' The answer is found in verse 18: 'Thou shalt not be afraid of them, but shalt well remember what the LORD thy God did unto Pharaoh, and unto all Egypt.' If this war becomes big, you can be sure that you will see me there without even being called."

The officer then said, "It is good that we met one another because I have learned much that will be of great benefit to me in the days ahead. Also, we have learned a lot about you and others like you, who before we always thought of as negative, but we know that two negatives always make a positive."

I was grateful to the Lord for the opportunity to meet with these military people and change their minds about true believers, especially at a time such as this, when any one of us could meet our end at any time.

—1982

## HOW CAN WE BELIEVE IN JESUS
## AND STILL SAY THAT WE ARE JEWS?

Here in this land from which the Word of God first came forth, it is especially important to preach the gospel of the Lord to those who are so deaf. Oh, they are not physically deaf, but they hate to hear the truth about the Lord. They hear only what they want to hear. Unfortunately, Jerusalem is not New York, and you cannot speak to Jews in Jerusalem as freely as you would speak to Jews in other parts of the world.

After living in Israel for 36 years, I am known by many people. Some, when they meet me, use the familiar greeting of all Israelis—"Shalom!"—and they are friendly toward me, even though they know that I believe in the Lord. Others have also known me for a long time, yet when they meet me they say something like, "Are you still alive? People like you would be better off dead!"

When I received one such greeting recently, I replied, "No, my dear, that is not so." "Don't you call me *dear*!" he shouted. "I am not your friend." I said, "You are not my friend now, but perhaps tomorrow you will be." "Never!" he responded. "You are an apostate, and I am a Jew. How can we be friends?" I told him, "For this reason it is written, 'I shall not die, but live, and declare the works of the LORD' [Ps. 118:17]." "What can you, a Christian, possibly tell me about the Lord?" he asked.

I saw this as a good opening and said, "The Lord created all people in His image. We are all equal, and we all have the same rights." "How do you know this?" he asked, and I replied, "I believe in the Lord, and He has given me things I never had before—salvation, love, and peace in my heart. All of these things I received through His Holy Spirit. I know that hearing words like these is a shock to people such as yourself, because you do not know about the Holy Spirit or being born again. It is for this reason that the Lord has kept me alive—through the Holocaust and four wars here in Israel—so that I can tell you and others like you of His mighty deeds to all people of the world. From this land, the Word of the Lord has gone forth to all nations of the earth."

He then asked, "Do you presume to tell me what to believe? You want me to accept this new faith that you believe in. You want me to believe in your Jesus." I responded, "You have believed a grave mistake for a very long time. The Lord Jesus did not come to make a new faith. He came to give us everlasting life."

That was more than this man could tolerate, and he asked if I suffered from a mental illness. I answered, "In time we shall know who suffers from a mental illness, and you shall also know that it is not my duty to compete with you to determine who is more wise. In the Talmud it is written, 'You sages, give heed to your words.' And the prophet wrote, 'Thus saith the LORD, Let not the wise man glory in his wisdom' [Jer. 9:23]. I can speak with you as an equal because we belong to the same Father, and a father does not show partiality among his children."

"No, we are not equal," he said, "because you believe in a different faith than I do." Again I told him, "The Lord did not come to make a new faith. He came to give us everlasting life through His suffering on our behalf." "Oh, yes, I know all about His suffering," he said sarcastically. "He simply died, and everyone knows that when a man is dead, he is dead. He has no more value." I then asked, "Would you like me to read about His suffering and what it accomplished?" "All right," he agreed, so I opened my Bible to Isaiah 53, the chapter that the Jews are not permitted to study and which they call "the forbidden chapter." As I read to him, starting with Isaiah 52:10, I was surprised to see how this one who was so sure of himself was now so interested in hearing about the Lord.

I can truly say that every day I see the truth in Jeremiah 17:7: "Blessed is the man who trusteth in the LORD, and whose hope the LORD is." This man who had been so antagonistic toward me and had even called me unkind names was now, thank the Lord, beginning to speak with me as a friend, even though he was still far from understanding the truth about the Lord. I realize that such people have spent their entire lives never having heard that truth. They know only what they have been told by their revered rabbis and what they have read in their many books of tradition handed down from generation to generation. It is from these sources that they have received their instruction in faith, and it has become holy to them. When I come to such people and give them facts from the Bible, they become curious and want to know more about the Lord. It is all so new to them, and, of course, all people are interested in something new. It is important to make them understand that Christians do not believe in a new faith, as they have been told. We don't believe in other gods, but in the one true God.

Because this man and I were talking in a public place, from time to time other people came past and listened in. Some even wanted to take part in the discussion. Everyone wants to prove himself more wise than the next person, and in such a discussion you will hear many interesting points made.  For instance, one man said, "Israel is not the right place for a Christian.  If you want to speak about Jesus, go to Europe or some other place in the world, but do not do it here in Israel!"  Following his comment, I asked the entire group, "Do you know where the first information about the Lord came from?"  They began to look at one another very uncomfortably, and no one said a word.  They were all as quiet as fish.  Finally, someone said, "Since you asked the question, you must know the answer."  I told them, "The first information about the Lord came from your own Holy Bible."  "No!  No!  That is not true!" they all shouted together, like a mixed chorus.  I then told them, "I have not held a gun to your heads and told you that you must receive the Lord.  If you say that you believe in the Holy Bible but you do not believe every word that is written there, you are making a big mistake.  You must follow the Lord according to the Bible, or you cannot call yourselves good Jews."  Again they sounded like a great chorus as they said, "How can we believe in Jesus and still say that we are Jews?"

I asked them, "Are you going to believe what you read in the Bible or what you read in the books written by the rabbis?  You can see for yourselves how many different ideas and opinions are contained in those many books.  How do you know which rabbi is right?  And who is a complete Jew—the one who has spent his whole life studying books filled with superstitions, or the one who believes in the Lord according to the Holy Bible?"  They were all very unhappy to hear the truth from an apostate such as I.

Then these men started a discussion among themselves, and it was pitiful to hear.  They were like blind people groping around in the darkness, and there was no one to lead they out to the light because they were all so hardhearted.  I had never met people with such deep hatred for those of us who believe in the Lord Jesus.  They kept repeating, "Jesus came to make a new faith, and because you believe in Him you have left the faith of our fathers."  Again I told them that Jesus did not come to make a new faith, but, rather, He came to save us and to give us everlasting life. I said, "If you would look at the Bible, instead of at your books of tradition, you would see this very clearly."

One of them said, "You are talking about the New Testament, but that does not belong to our Holy Bible." I told him, "That is another point about which you are mistaken. Jeremiah 31:31 says, 'Behold, the days come, saith the LORD, that I will make a new covenant with the house of Israel, and with the house of Judah.' The term *New Testament*, which is so hated by the people of this nation, is actually the Hebrew phrase *brith Hadasha* and is the new covenant referred to by Jeremiah. Jesus said 'Think not that I am come to destroy the law, or the prophets; I am not come to destroy, but to fulfill. For verily I say unto you, Till heaven and earth pass, one jot or one tittle shall in no way pass from the law, till all be fulfilled' [Mt. 5:17-18].

"You can see from this the great difference between what you have been taught and what Jesus actually said to His followers when He walked in this very land. You have been brainwashed by your false teachers. Satan has gained entrance and is dancing among you, and you with him. You are filled with vanity, and from this comes many evil things, such as superstition, slander, and talebearing, which the Lord speaks against in Leviticus 19:16: 'Thou shalt not go up and down as a talebearer among thy people.'"

I was surprised to see that all these people were listening closely to what I was saying, so I asked, "Now what do you think about all of this? Do you still think the Lord Jesus came to make a new faith? Or do you now realize that He came to fulfill all that was written in the Old Testament Scriptures? He came to give us that which we had lost—faith. Without faith in the Lord, we are lost forever."

They replied, "Whether we like it or not, we must admit that you are right. We are sorry about what has happened here today."

I told them, "I am not sorry, but happy. Through such a discussion we can learn much and come to a true understanding of the Lord. Also, you can see that even though just a short time ago you were my sworn enemies, now, through the love of the Lord, we can speak together as friends. If you will strive to learn more about the Lord and His great love for all people, then you will be able to stand against the false teachers who abound in our midst, and the glory of the Lord will be revealed in you." They all said together just one short word, "Amen," and I said, "Amen" also.

—1984

# EVERY CLOUD HAS A SILVER LINING

I was recently asked to visit an elderly man whose son is my friend. When I arrived at his home, I could immediately see that he was very sick and that I had arrived in the last hours of his life. He had refused to talk to anyone, even his children, but when I entered his room he seemed happy, although I am sure he knew that this would be his last day on earth.

He told me that he had been a drunk all of his life, and now the end had come for him. He said, "Now that I have reached the end of my life, I realize that I have never known satisfaction—not from things, not from people, not even from my children. And now I will be lost forever, and it will be just as if I had never lived on this earth." He then went on to say, "I know with whom I am speaking. I know that you do not believe as I do, but it is written in the Talmud, 'A man does not lie on his deathbed.' I know that it is my own fault that I will be forever lost because I have been very bad and drank far too much. I never thought about my family—the bottle was the most important thing in my life. And now I am sure that not even God Himself will hear my voice if I call upon Him.”

I told him, “No, my dear friend, that is not so.  As we always say, every cloud has a silver lining, and you can truly have a silver lining because even now, in the last moments of your life, you can be saved.”  “What did you say?” he asked.  “Can I be saved after everything I have done in my life?”  “Yes,” I answered.  “The Lord, our Savior, is so good that He came and gave Himself for us all, so that we never have to die but can live forever.  We can have everlasting life.”

He closed his eyes and became so quiet that I thought perhaps he had died.  But no, he was just thinking.  When he opened his eyes, he told me that he was very interested in what I had said.  He asked who had told me these things and if they were really true.  “If what you have said is true,” he said, “then there is hope for me to be saved, even after the terrible life I have led.”  I told him that everything I had said was indeed true, and just to reassure him, I read Isaiah 53:6:  “All we like sheep have gone astray; we have turned every one to his own way, and the LORD hath laid on him the iniquity of us all.”  I then said, “This passage, from our own Hebrew Scriptures, is meant for everyone who comes to the Lord, even if that happens at the very end of a person’s life.  God is good, and anyone who comes to Him in the name of our Savior can be sure that he will not be lost.  All you have to do is put your trust in Him.  It is also written in John 3:16, ‘For God so loved the world, that he gave his only begotten Son, that whosoever believeth in him should not perish, but have everlasting life.’ ”

I was surprised to see this man become so peaceful and quiet.  When his son came into the room, he could not believe what he saw and asked, “What have you done to my father that he is so quiet and says he is happy?”  I replied, “You must ask your father.”  When he did so, his father related to him everything he had heard and said that he believed it.  The son was not pleased and asked, “How could you do this to my father at such a time as this?" I told him, "It is my duty, and the duty of everyone who believes in the Lord as his Savior, to come to other people in their time of need and help them see the truth. Otherwise, they will be lost, as your father was. We are responsible for each other."

"How can you be responsible for my father?" he asked. "You are not a member of this family." I replied, "We have one Father in heaven, and we are one family in Him. As members of His family, we have a responsibility to one another. This is made very clear in Ezekiel 33:7-8, where it is written, 'So thou, O son of man, I have set thee a watchman unto the house of Israel; therefore, thou shalt hear the word at my mouth, and warn them from me. When I say unto the wicked, O wicked man, thou shalt surely die; if thou dost not speak to warn the wicked from his way, that wicked man shall die in his iniquity, but his blood will I require at thine hand.' Do you think it is against the law for me to speak as I did to your father? Why, just look at him now. There is no fear on his face, even though he knows this may be his last day in this life. He has received great courage to do that which the Lord requires of us, and I think you can tell by looking at his face that the Lord has given him peace by receiving him through His providence. Are you against your father having such peace in his last hours?"

"No," the son replied, "but I am against you because you spoke with my father about a faith that he never heard about all through his life." "That is just the point," I said. "Even though he had not heard before how to have true faith in the Lord, the Lord is still willing to receive him, and your father is happy because he knows that he is no longer lost. He is now saved, and you can see that he is happy and peaceful in the last moments of his life. This can be a great example for your family. You will all have to stand before the Lord one day, just as your father will do very soon. He was bitter and melancholy because of the problems alcohol had caused him.

He told me that he has never been happy in his entire life. But now, at the very end of his life, he has found happiness and has peace in his heart because, for the first time, he has heard the truth about the Lord Jesus Christ and has gladly received what he heard. He is not drunk now; his mind is very clear, and he is happy in the Lord. Now you and the rest of your family can come into his room and share his last moments with him in happiness."

This was for me a very thrilling day, but it was also a very sad day. It was thrilling because this man accepted the Lord as his Savior, and he will spend eternity with Him in heaven. It was a sad day because I know that even though his family was happy that their father had found peace at the end of his life, they have not accepted for themselves the Savior who gave this peace to their father. I pray that they will think about what happened to him and that they will accept the Lord soon, before they reach their deathbeds in a lost and hopeless condition.

—1986

# WHERE DID I GO ASTRAY?

"Who is like unto thee, O LORD, among the gods?" (Ex. 15:11). Not many people know this truth; therefore, they live their lives hoping that better times will come. They live in fear of the situations that surround them. Others, however, are not anxious because they have put their trust in the Lord. I am among this latter group, and so I sleep well and am happy because I am sure of the one in whom I believe.

While walking on the streets of Jerusalem one day, I met a man who seemed very familiar to me. I soon realized that we had served together in the army in 1948 but had not seen each other since. Although we had both changed in physical appearance over 38 years, David's first words were, "Zvi, you have not changed. You seem as happy as ever." He, however, seemed far from happy, and I was afraid to ask the reason. Then he said, "Come with me to a quiet place, and I will tell you why I am so unhappy." I replied, "Let's go to my home, where it is quiet and peaceful. There we can talk at length."

After dinner, David spoke of his real concern. "I am sad and anxious because two of my sons are in the army. Can you understand this?" he asked. "No," I replied. "I cannot understand it as a cause for your depression, for I have three sons in the army, all in combat units." He found this hard to believe, since my face did not show great concern. "How can you be so calm about it?" he asked. "I would like to know the secret of your happiness." I spoke to him about the words of Psalm 3—about putting our trust in God. "This is my secret for enduring troubles."

David then asked, "How can I put my trust in God when I have so many problems in my life?" I reminded him that even as Abraham was tempted and tried, yet remained strong, so we must be strong to withstand the trials we face. "You can do this, David, by putting your trust in the Lord, our Savior," I told him. He was surprised at my answer and asked, "Are you a rabbi now?" "No," I replied, "but I do believe in the Lord. Therefore, I have a duty to preach the gospel, and now it is your privilege to hear it." As I told him of my concern for his well-being, I explained that I too had once been unhappy, bitter, and no longer wanted to live. However, from the time that I received the Lord into my heart, there was no more despair—only joy!

As David looked at the pictures of my sons, he began to question himself: *What is the matter with me? Am I normal? Do I have some kind of complex?* Finally he asked, "Where did I go astray? Can you tell me?" Anticipating this question, I answered, "Yes, I can tell you. First, you must realize that God Himself is always ready to help us, and you can pray to Him. As it is written, 'therefore will I call upon him as long as I live' [Ps. 116:2]." I told him, "God can help you, and now is the time!"

He was interested to know how I had come to believe as I do, and I was delighted to give him my testimony. Then I began to read the words of John 3:16, but he shouted, "No! This is not the Bible, it is a Christian book—the New Testament. If you want to read, read only from the Jewish Scriptures." I explained to him that the Lord Jesus Christ is mentioned not only in the New Testament, but in the whole Bible.

David lives far from Jerusalem, so we invited him to spend the night with us. This gave me further opportunity to witness to him, all the while praying that he would come to know the Lord and be as happy as we are.

When he left our home the next day, he said, "Thank you. I have a very special feeling within me now. I wish it could last." "My dear brother," I said, "this can be yours forever. You now know my secret. As you have thanked me, be sure to thank the Lord as well."

David departed from our home with much to consider. I pray that his "very special feeling" will lead him to genuinely commit his life to God and that he will grow in grace and in the knowledge of the Lord Jesus Christ.

—1986

# IT IS HARD FOR US TO FORSAKE
# THE OLD WAYS

The Bible states in many places that the people of Israel are God's *Chosen People*, His *peculiar treasure.* Israelis today consider this to be a great honor, but most forget that there are conditions involved for them to receive God's blessings as His Chosen People. In Deuteronomy 11:26-28 the Lord said, "Behold, I set before you this day a blessing and a curse: A blessing, if ye obey the commandments of the LORD your God, which I command you this day; And a curse, if ye will not obey the commandments of the LORD your God, but turn aside out of the way which I command you this day, to go after other gods, which ye have not known."

If the people obey the Lord and keep His commandments, He will bless them. If they do not obey Him but do evil, He will curse them. I am sure no one wants to be cursed, but there are many people in Israel who believe that because we are the Chosen People, God will only do good for us. They feel that they do not have to obey the Lord and keep His commandments, that the very fact that they live in Israel is the same as doing the greatest of good deeds for the Lord.

I recently met some people who believe this way, and I told them, "My friends, it is not enough that you live in Israel. It is written in Deuteronomy 12:1, 'These are the statutes and ordinances which ye shall observe to do in the land, which the LORD God of thy fathers giveth thee to possess, all the days that ye live upon the earth.' Because we are the Chosen People, we must be an example to the rest of the world. We must not continue to believe the fantasy that just because we live in Israel, we are free to do whatever we like."

One man asked, "Do you not think it is a great thing that the people of Israel spend so many years studying the Talmud?" "No," I replied. Then he challenged, "Show me any other nation on earth whose people have studied their holy books for as many years as the people of Israel have studied the Talmud." I told him, "It is sad that even with all your studying, you are so far from the truth." They were surprised to hear this and began to ask among themselves, "Who is this man? Is he normal?" I assured them that I was indeed normal, and I told them, "You can spend all your lives studying your holy books, but the Lord will consider it nothing more than vanity."

Then they asked, "Are you courageous enough to go to the rabbis and tell them what you are telling us? We realize that you are a Christian, and you want us to receive Jesus as our 'Savior,' as you people always say. We are sure that you will not tell this to the rabbis because you are afraid of them." "Never!" I replied. "Everyone must be told the truth about our Savior, and, as a matter of fact, on many occasions I have spoken with rabbis and told them what I just told you. In reality, it is you who are afraid of the rabbis. They do not have horns; they do not bite. You can speak your mind to them. I know this may not seem like a simple thing to do, but, as we always say, where there is a will there is a way, and that way is open to everyone. You can see that I am perfectly free to witness among people who have never heard about the Lord Jesus. You must realize that one day, when you stand before the Lord to give an account of what you have done here on earth, your rabbis will not stand with you. You will stand before Him alone. Neither do the rabbis have the power to forgive your sins."

I could tell that they were beginning to take an interest in what I was sharing, but one of the men said, "I am sure you know how many years and for how many generations we have followed the traditions of our fathers and revered the rabbis. It is hard for us to forsake the old ways. Our fathers lived and died following these traditions." "I understand your concerns," I told them, "but if you do not change your ways, when you die you will be lost forever with no opportunity to be saved."

When they heard this, they appeared to be frightened and asked, "Do you think we have already gone too far? Do you think we are lost already?" "No," I answered. "In fact, this is only the beginning for you. When you start to fear, your eyes will be open to see the clear truth as it is presented in the Bible. You will see the folly of following after the old traditions of your fathers and teachers and not accepting the responsibility for your eternal souls."

One of the men said, "You don't have to tell us that. We have studied the Talmud all our lives. You cannot teach us anything that we do not already know." At that point I said to the entire group, "Please put your hands on your hearts and tell me truthfully, which book is more important—the Talmud, or the Torah, the book of the law that we received on Mount Sinai? If you are such good Jews, why don't you keep the law as it is written in Deuteronomy 5:7, 'Thou shalt have no other gods before me'? This is only one of the many commandments of God that the people of Israel—the Chosen People—do not keep. Deuteronomy 6:4 says, 'Hear, O Israel: The LORD our God is one LORD.' Where are your ears, that you may hear? The Bible clearly tells us that every person is responsible for him or herself before the Lord, and Ezekiel 18:20 tells us, 'The soul that sinneth, it shall die.' From this passage we can see that not even our fathers in the flesh can help us, and surely the rabbis cannot save us. They are here with us today, but tomorrow they will be in another place. But God is everlasting, and He will never leave you. If you will receive the Lord your God, then you will be blessed rather than cursed."

At the end of this very long conversation, one of these people said, "We are surprised by what you have shared with us. We never realized that those who believe in Jesus follow the Bible so closely. This is the first time we have spoken freely with someone like you and the first time we have heard what you really believe."

I am praying for these people who, until now, never heard the good news of salvation in Jesus Christ. Unfortunately, there are so many more like them in the land of Israel. I pray that the believers in this land—although we are certainly a minority—will be used by the Lord to reach many of His Chosen People with the gospel. As I told them, there must always be a beginning. I pray for them and many others who will hear for the first time, that the Lord will cause them to meditate on what they hear, that they will recognize the truth as it is written in His Word, and that they will open their hearts to Him as their Savior and Messiah.

—1987

# A PACKAGE OF GOOD DEEDS—
# OR MISDEEDS?

I recently was walking along the street in the old city of Jerusalem, and I saw two young Orthodox Jewish students carrying what appeared to be a very heavy package. It was so big that every few minutes the boys would stop and put down the package so they could rest before going on. After watching them for a while, I approached them and asked if I could help. They didn't answer, but when I asked what was in the heavy package they answered, "This is a package of good deeds." I was sure that it must contain clothing or food for poor people, and so I commended them saying, "That certainly is a good deed. May the Lord bless you." After all, they were young boys, and they deserved to be commended for doing a good deed.

Then one of the boys asked, "Do you know what is in this big package?" "Clothing or food for poor people," I responded. "Oh no!" they said. "What we have here is very holy. They are the books of commentaries for the Ultra-Orthodox students." When I heard that I said, "If you were to ask me now what is in your package, I would tell you that it is a big package of misdeeds." "How can you say that about the roots of our faith?" they asked. I responded with another question: "What part does the law have in our lives? I am referring to the law that we received from God through Moses on Mount Sinai. Which is more important for us, that law or the so-called laws contained in your heavy package?"

"You have asked a very hard question," one boy said, "and we cannot answer it. But, if you want an answer, come with us. If you would like, you may help us carry our books along the way. We will go to see our rabbis, and we are sure they will give you the right answer to your question." I agreed to go with them, and as we walked along, I had a good opportunity to share the Word of God with them.

We finally arrived at their yeshiva—their *holy of holies*—and the students said to their rabbi, "This man helped us to carry these heavy books." The rabbi was very appreciative and thanked me. Then the students said, "This kind man has also asked us a question that we cannot answer, and so we would like you to answer him." The rabbi said, "I will be happy to answer any question that pertains to our faith. What would you like to know?"

I asked, "Rabbi, why do you spend all your life and encourage your young students to spend their lives studying these books that have no value—no value for you, for these young boys, and certainly no value for God?" "Who are you, to speak to me like this?" he demanded. "Do you have anything further to say?" "Yes," I replied. "I am very sorry to see such young boys following after false teachings. It is true that we are a very wise people, but, on the other side of the coin, we are in many ways more backward than any other nation on earth."

"You are speaking in riddles," the rabbi said. "Give me a clear explanation of what you mean." I then took out the small Bible that I always carry with me and said, "You don't even know what is written in this book." He replied, "There is so much written in it that I don't know what you want me to tell you." I said, "In Deuteronomy 6:16-17 it is written, 'Ye shall not put the LORD your God to the test, as ye tested him in Massah. Ye shall diligently keep the commandments of the LORD your God, and his testimonies, and his statutes, which he hath commanded thee.' But what are you doing? Instead of keeping God's commandments, you have taken upon yourself a great, heavy burden that has no value. You have invested your entire life in the study of commentaries that have been passed down by men from generation to generation; but the Word of God, which is so holy, you have cast away. What's more, you have tested God because what you are doing is against His will. If you would read the truth found in the Bible, you would realize that you have wasted your life."

By this time several other people had gathered around and were listening to our conversation. They began to take part in the discussion, but they were not very polite to me. Their first question was, "Are you a *meshumed* [*apostate*]?" "No! I have been a complete Jew since the time I came to know the Lord according to the way He has instructed us in the Bible, His Holy Word. I am sorry for you because you have been living in such deep darkness. And, what's more, you are taking others with you. These young boys could be saved, but because of you they will be lost. As we say, when the shepherd strays, the sheep will stray after him; and you have all gone astray. But there is a way to escape the darkness and come into the light." I then read for them the 53rd chapter of Isaiah, emphasizing verse 6: "All we like sheep have gone astray; we have turned every one to his own way." I then said, "Now tell me, who are the apostates? It cannot be those of us who believe what is written in Deuteronomy 6:14, 'Ye shall not go after other gods, of the gods of the people who are round about you.' "

This was too much for them, and one man said, "We are Jews,

but you are not a Jew because you believe in another god." I asked, "How is it possible for one who believes and follows all that is written in the Bible to believe in another god? Never! I have shown you living facts from God's own Word—facts to prove that it is you who are the apostates. If you will take up your books again, this time with an open mind and heart before the Lord, He will show you the folly of your beliefs."

They all became very quiet, and after a while I said, "Since you do not seem to have anything more to say, let me read again for you Deuteronomy 6:16: 'Ye shall not put the LORD your God to the test.' If you put your trust in the Lord, and in Him alone, He will give you what you can never receive by devoting your lives to studying these false teachings. Think about this." "You have certainly given us much to think about," they admitted.

I pray that these students, along with their rabbis and teachers, will close their books of commentaries and traditions and open God's Word, which alone has the answers to all the questions of life, and through which they can find the real way to God and the salvation He freely gives to all who receive His Son and our Messiah, the Lord Jesus.

—1987

## ZVI IS STRICKEN WITH A HEART ATTACK
## WHILE WALKING IN JERUSALEM

Believers are all one family in the Lord, and I experienced this family-type closeness and concern recently.  On February 27, I suffered a very serious heart attack as I was walking along the street in Jerusalem.  I was rushed unconscious to the hospital, where I remained unconscious for more than 24 hours.  The doctors told my family that I was clinically dead and there was no hope for my recovery.  Further, they said that if I did survive—which they doubted—I would be helpless and useless, and my memory would be gone.

Of course, my wife and children were worried, but they did not lose hope.  The put their trust in the Lord and began to pray.  They also notified many of our brothers and sisters in the Lord, and believers in Israel, the United States, and many other countries began to pray for me.  They were all one family united in believing prayer before our Lord and Savior, and He was pleased to honor their faith.  After three days, I was so greatly improved that all life-support equipment was disconnected, and in another week I was discharged from the hospital.

I realize that I was very close to my everlasting home, but I can truly say that I was at peace because I knew where I would be if my earthly life ended. This was not the first time I had faced death, having been in many dangerous and life-threatening situations during the Holocaust in Europe and in the wars here in Israel. They say that a cat has nine lives, but I am sure that if I were in competition with a cat, it would lose! I am happy to say, along with our Lord Jesus, "Father, into thy hands I commend my spirit" (Lk. 23:46). I am always ready to meet my God. The Lord has said, "be thou faithful unto death, and I will give thee a crown of life" (Rev. 2:10). We also read in Amos 4:12, "prepare to meet thy God." I truly thank the Lord that at a time when I was close to death, I was prepared to meet Him. I had someone to whom I could open my heart, someone I knew would welcome me to my eternal home.

I was surprised and gratified by the many people, some of whom I had never met, who came to the hospital and told my family and me, "Don't worry; everything will be fine. We are praying for you, and we are sure the Lord will answer our prayers." I know that everything that was accomplished on my behalf was through the faith of my dear family and my many, many brothers and sisters in the Lord, both in Israel and around the world. I am so grateful to Him and to everyone who showed their love and concern for me. It is written, "without faith it is impossible to please him" (Heb. 11:6). I praise the Lord for the faith of my family and friends and for His power, which worked a miracle in my life.

While I was in the hospital, I shared a room with a man who was 80 years old, and he too had many visitors. Most of them spoke German, but one man asked me in Hebrew, "What is your position?" "Why do you ask that?" I inquired. "Surely you must know that when we get to our everlasting home, no one will ask what position we held on earth. We will not be judged according to our standing in society." He then asked, "What type of work do you do?" "I am a carpenter," I replied. When he heard that, he made a sour face and asked the other visitors in German, "Do you think it is possible for our loved one to change rooms?"

Of course, I understood what he said, and I responded in German, "You are free to do whatever you like, but you should realize that it is not possible to make a contract with God assuring that you will always be in high society. God is no respecter of persons. He does not care if you are rich or poor. Everyone will have to stand before Him in judgment, and we will each stand alone."

The old gentleman in the bed seemed very happy to hear what I was saying, but his family was not quite so happy. One of them asked if I had graduated from a university or other secondary school, along with many other similar questions. I told him, "It is written in Psalm 111:10, 'The fear of the LORD is the beginning of wisdom,' but this wisdom is very far from you." They did not know how to respond to this, and it was difficult for them to accept, since they were all university graduates and I was a mere carpenter.

They then began to question me in another direction. "Do you read books or special literature, such as Shakespeare?" I replied, "I know that Shakespeare wrote, 'To be, or not to be? That is the question.' But the only true question is, 'To be?' You will not find the answer to that question in Shakespeare. For the answers to the questions of life and death, you must look in the only book that can impart to you the wisdom of God. The nation of Israel was divinely intended to be an example to the nations of the world, but, sadly, we read many times in the book to which I referred that we are not fulfilling our divine obligation. For instance, it is written, 'Wherefore should the nations say, Where is now their God?' [Ps. 115:2]. And again, 'Why should they say among the people, Where is their God?' [Joel 2:17]. We are the Chosen People of God, and yet, as a nation, we spend most of our time pursuing emptiness. You have been trying to impress me with your great honor and position in society, but this book also has something to say about people like yourselves: 'For when he dieth he shall carry nothing away; his glory shall not descend after him' [Ps. 49:17]."

They had become very interested in what I was saying, and after a long conversation they asked, "Can you show us this book, so that we will know from where you have read all of this?" I now faced a hard decision. The hospital was a very religious, Orthodox institution, and I knew it would be upsetting for these people to see the New Testament there, of all places. I silently prayed, "Oh Lord, open their blind eyes so that they can see the truth." By then it was 1 a.m., and we still had not finished our discussion. They were so interested to know more, but they never expected that in this hospital, this veritable *holy of holies*, they would see the New Testament. As soon as I showed it to them, they all said, "You are a Christian!" "I am a better Jew than any of you," I replied. "But you have brought a Christian book into this religious place," they protested. "When the rabbi comes tomorrow, we will tell him that you want to make us Christians."

I responded, "You are free to tell the rabbi whatever you like, but you should remind him that he spends a lot time reading the Bible, and the New Testament is an important part of the Bible. You can see the close relationship between the Old and New Testaments by comparing just a few passages. For example, we read in Isaiah 40:3, 'The voice of him that crieth in the wilderness, Prepare ye the way of the LORD, make straight in the desert a highway for our God.' And now listen to what the New Testament says in Mark 1:2-3: 'Behold, I send my messenger before thy face, who shall prepare thy way before thee. The voice of one crying in the wilderness, Prepare ye the way of the Lord, make his paths straight.' This is in perfect accord with the Old Testament, and I pray you will ask your rabbi about it when he comes tomorrow.

"Your rabbi teaches you the old stories that were written through the centuries by other rabbis, telling of the great things that they did in their lives, but you have seen the truth from God's Word. Now you must choose between the truth of God and the traditions the rabbis tell you. The Word of God exhorts us to be examples to the other nations of the world, and, as you know, many people from all around the world come to Israel to see for themselves the Chosen People of God. And what do they see? The same 'stiff-necked people' that Israel has always been. Tell this to your rabbi when he comes for a visit tomorrow."

I believe strongly in Paul's words to the believers in Rome: "And we know that all things work together for good to them that love God, to them who are the called according to his purpose" (Rom. 8:28). As a result of my heart attack, I was given the opportunity to witness to doctors, nurses, patients, yes, and even the rabbi in the midst of the Orthodox Jewish hospital. Some were disinterested; others said, "We will discuss these things with you again." The seed of the Word was planted in hearts, and now I pray that it will take root, grow, and bear eternal fruit.

—1987

## ALWAYS PREPARED

As believers in the Lord Jesus Christ, we must "be diligent in season, out of season" (2 Tim. 4:2) and "be ready always to give an answer to every man that asketh you a reason of the hope that is in you, with meekness and fear" (1 Pet. 3:15). We must always be prepared to witness for Him because we never know whom the Lord may choose to bring across our paths.

So it was in my home recently, and I must say that this was an exceptional situation. A lady came to visit, and it was not the first time she had come to speak with me. She was one of my daughter's high school teachers, and she lives in our neighborhood. For several years she has visited us from time to time. We always welcome her gladly, and she is very kind to us, even though she knows that we believe in Jesus as our Savior. But this time, it was not just a social call. This time she wanted to know about our faith and asked many questions. Of course, I was happy to answer her and tell her about Christ. She said, "I want to know more about Him and how you came to believe in Him." I was delighted to give her my testimony, and I encouraged her to visit us as often as she liked. I told her, "It may be that in time the Lord will open your eyes and your heart to Him." "But what can I do by myself to come closer to Him?" she asked. I replied, "We can talk together, learn together, and pray together, and the Lord will do what we cannot do for ourselves."

I was pleased that she continued to visit me, and each time she asked if I knew others who believed in the Lord and how they had come to believe in Him. One day I asked, "Are you here to draw closer to the Lord or to investigate me?" She answered, very sincerely, "I appreciate our talks together. You are always very pleasant to me, and I do enjoy coming to your home. I am sure this will not be my last visit because I am truly interested in knowing how you came to your faith in the Lord. I would really like to know the one who brought you to this faith." "Since you seem genuinely interested," I responded, "I will be glad to tell you about the one who led me to the Lord." I then gave her a Bible and said, "Take this home and read it. As you do, pray to the Lord and ask Him to be your guide, to show you the way to come to Himself. As He guided and directed me in my search for Him, I am sure He will do the same for you." She accepted the Bible and left.

But that was not the end. About five hours later, her husband knocked on my door. "I have nothing against you," he assured me as I invited him in, "but please do not give my wife any more of this poison," he said as he handed me the Bible I had given her. I asked, "Do you believe in God?" "Yes," he replied, "but not in the way you want my wife to believe." I then told him, "I only want to help her find the truth according to the Holy Scriptures. If this is poison, then tell me, what is the truth? In what can we believe, if not in the Bible and in the living God who is described in its pages?"

He was far from happy and said, "To be perfectly honest, I do not really believe in God—I never have. And now you want me to believe in Jesus? Are you crazy? Let me tell you about my work, which I am sure will surprise you. I work against Christian missionaries in Israel and against all Jews like you who believe in Jesus—the apostates! Yes, this is my job, and I am very happy doing it. I am happy to fight against all of you who try to make the Jewish people accept a new religion."

"If this is so," I said, "then you have come to the right place. You can fight against me!" "Oh no," he said, "I would never fight against you because we are neighbors. What's more, you have been a good friend over the years." I told him, "What you are saying is very nice, but you must remember that I did not come to you or your wife and ask you to believe in me. I am just a human being, like any other person on the face of this earth. I am not eternal, and I am helpless to save myself or anyone else from sin. But, I can help you to know the Lord, our Savior. I can be a fescue—a pointer—pointing you to a true knowledge of God according to the Bible, His Holy Word."

I then said, "If you think what I am doing is against the law, feel free to bring to my home other members of your organization, other people who are fighting so hard against believers in the Lord Jesus. But remember what the Prophet Isaiah wrote: 'Behold, the LORD's hand is not shortened, that it cannot save; neither his ear heavy, that it cannot hear' [Isa. 59:1]. It may be that the Lord will enable your friends to believe what you refuse to believe. If you would like to come back with your friends, you may be sure that I will not run away before you get here. I am ready to face them. As a matter of fact, I am willing to go with you to your office right now, and I will give a good report of you to your superiors. I will tell them that you are doing your job very well. Why, you may even be promoted!"

He then became very serious and said, "Don't you realize that you could be killed if I did what you are suggesting, especially if I tell them you tried to make my wife a Christian. Are you sure you want me to bring my friends here?" "Yes," I replied, "but I want you to know that I will not be alone." "Who would dare to join you at such a time?" he asked. "I am sure no one would be that crazy!" I then reminded him what God said to Abraham, Jacob, Moses, and all of His servants. He told them not to fear because He would be with them and would protect them. "And so it will be with me," I assured him. "At a time when I will be among wolves, the Lord will be at my side, and I will not be afraid."

He said, "You may not be afraid, but I am. If I tell these people that because you are my neighbor I don't really fight against you, I will probably lose my job." "I have lost my job many times because of my faith in the Lord," I told him, "and I have been in more serious, even dangerous situations than I can remember. However, I have never lost my hope in the Lord because He has told us in His Word, 'be not afraid of them [our enemies]' [Dt. 20:1]."

This man then left my home, and I wondered what would happen next. I didn't have to wonder for long because the next day his wife visited me again. She seemed more self-confident and sure of herself than she ever had in the past. I asked, "Are you not afraid to come here? Don't you know what your husband told me? He plans to fight against me because of my faith in the Lord." She replied, "I have no fear. My husband knows where I am and what I am doing here, and he told me not to be afraid because he will not inform his superiors about you. Now, please tell me more. I want to know about the Lord!"

I praise God for this woman—for her courage, her interest in the Lord, and her desire to know more about Him. I am praying that very soon she will come to know Him as her Messiah and Savior. I am also praying for her husband. It is possible that he is under strong conviction from the Lord and that he may one day yield his life to Him. In the interim, we will pray for his safety among those with whom he works on a daily basis.

—1987

# HOW CAN GOD HAVE A BIRTHDAY?

In the days preceding Christmas, many people in Israel ask believers, "How can God have a birthday?" The concept of the birth of Jesus is very hard for the Jewish people to accept. I am always asked during the Christmas season, "Why do you want the Jews to be partners in your fantasy and dance around the golden calf with the Christians?" Unfortunately, they never give me an opportunity to reply. I receive only attacks because, in their eyes, I am guilty of a great deception.

I recently said to a group of such people, "If you have any more questions, ask them now, and when you are finished I will answer you—but the answer may surprise you." Then they fired off a series of questions: "Why are you so happy at this time of the year?" "Why do you make such a big celebration on Christmas day?" "Who was really born on that day?" "Wasn't he only a man, a man named Jesus, a human being just like us?" "Why have you created such a fantasy about him?" "Who was this Jesus?" "Why did he come?"

When they had exhausted their list, I responded, "Now I will answer you, but let me begin by telling you a story. Once, on a very cold winter day, a man noticed a small bird outside his window. He realized that the bird wanted to come in and warm itself, but the window was closed. The man wanted to help the bird, so he opened the window to let it come in, but the poor bird became frightened and flew away. The man felt sorry for the bird and wished that he could become a bird so he could speak to the frightened creature and invite it into his home to get warm.

"The Jewish people are just like that poor bird," I told my listeners. "Our forefathers were afraid of what they could not see; therefore, they did not want to do what the Lord expected of them. But God loved them very much and did not want them to fly off on their own and be lost forever. And so, in His great mercy, He sent His own Son to us in the form of a man. His Son spoke with us in our own language, telling us what God was really like and how much He loved us. Then He suffered and died for us—in our place—so that we could be reconciled to God. Because of this, we can be happy in the Lord, we can sing and praise His holy name, especially around this time of year when we commemorate His coming from heaven to earth."

These people listened very intently and seemed interested, but when I finished one of them said. "That was a nice story, but it is only for Christians. There is nothing written in our Jewish Bible about Jesus." I replied, "I told you that you would receive a surprise when I answered your questions, and now I will show you that surprise. I will show you from the Jewish Scriptures one of the songs sung by Christians at this time of year to welcome our Lord and Savior, and we sing it in the Hebrew language." I then opened my Bible and read Zechariah 9:9: "Rejoice greatly, O daughter of Zion; shout, O daughter of Jerusalem; behold, thy King cometh unto thee; he is just, and having salvation."

I then continued, "We do not sing this on Christmas day just to keep alive a fantasy about a mere man. Jesus came from heaven to earth because mankind had sunk deep into sin, and there was no way for them to be saved. It was necessary for God to send Him—His only begotten Son—in the form of a man, so that mankind could get a clear picture of God and so that we could speak with Him face to face, as a loving father speaks with his children. On the Day of Atonement, we pray, 'Wash me thoroughly from mine iniquity, and cleanse me from my sin' [Ps. 51:2]. When the Lord Jesus came to earth and gave Himself for us, it was to cleanse us from our everlasting sin.

"At the beginning of our conversation you asked why Christians are so happy at Christmas. Now I ask you, why should we not be happy? The Lord has come; He has saved us by shedding His blood. If we accept His sacrifice on our behalf, we can be sure of spending eternity in heaven with Him."

Once again my listeners said, "This is only a Christian story, found in Christian books. It is not for the Jews." I countered by saying, "The stories that you hear from the rabbis are so old that they should have long beards by now, but they are only stories—false stories handed down from generation to generation. I want to hear something new from you. But, even more than that, I want to hear something that is based on the true and living Word of God, and not the stories you have received through the centuries from false teachers. Please examine the Scriptures for yourselves and open your minds and hearts to their teachings. Draw your own conclusions and do not rely on what the rabbis tell you. If you do this, then I will be glad to speak with you again."

I praise the Lord that they were open to my proposal, and one of the men said, "We are serious about this. Tell us the importance of the coming of the Messiah." I was thrilled at this response and said, "If you are truly interested, you can read about the coming of the Messiah in your own Jewish Bible. Such passages as Micah 5:2; Isaiah 7:14; 9:6-7, and the entire 53rd chapter of Isaiah will give you a clear picture of His coming and who He is. If you have the time, I will be glad to read these passages and discuss them with you, and I can show you many other passages pertaining to the Messiah."

I was delighted that they were willing to read the Scriptures with me, and when we were finished I asked, "Now do you understand why I am so happy in Him? Do you realize what a joy it is to glorify His holy name and sing praises to Him? Or do you need more proof? Is the Bible not enough? Do you think the stories of the rabbis are true and more relevant to the Messiah than what we have read from the Holy Scriptures?" "Oh no!" they said. "The Bible is the only book." "If that is so, what are you waiting for?" I asked. "Why not believe in your hearts all that we have read, and then you too can share in the joy of this season when we celebrate the coming of the Lord to the earth for the Jewish people and all other people of the world. Wouldn't you like to be happy about the birth of the Messiah?"

They all agreed that they were glad I had explained the significance of Christmas, and they promised to think carefully about all that I had told them and to read the Scripture passages again.

There are many people in the world, and each one has the privilege of being saved if he or she will come to the Lord according to the way He has ordained in His Word. Because of this, each person has the right to hear the good news of the incarnation of the Lord Jesus Christ and of His death and resurrection, which accomplished the forgiveness of sin, the salvation of the soul, and the assurance of eternity in heaven with Him for everyone who yields his or her life to the Savior. We cannot save people, but we can be guides and point others to the one who is "the light of the world" (Jn. 8:12).

—1987

## THE PRIVATE DETECTIVE

I live in an apartment-type building in Jerusalem, and all the residents own their own flats. We have a house committee to represent the residents, and for ten years I was a member of that committee. Over the years, I made many good friends among the residents. Often I was invited to their homes or I invited them to my home. During those ten years, we lived together as one big family, and I had good conversations with many of my neighbors about a variety of subjects, including my faith. I always gave them a clear explanation of what I believe and in whom I believe. The residents came to understand who I was and what I stood for, and because of my openness, many came to like me and were even sympathetic toward me when I was attacked by Ultra-Orthodox Jews because of my faith.

When my last term on the house committed was completed, I was replaced by a man who is a relatively new resident in the building. As we always say, "The king is dead. Long live the new king!" This new committee member soon began asking questions about all the residents—what kind of work they do, how they live, etc. He wanted to know things that did not concern him. Everyone began to say that he was like a private detective, and then we learned that he is a member of an Ultra-Orthodox religious group and was reporting to the group about all the residents in our building.

Eventually he got around to me and my family. Every month we pay a fee for maintenance, and he came to my home to collect this money. I could tell immediately that he is very nosy because as he walked through the door he began to ask questions: "How well do you live? Do you go to the synagogue on the Sabbath? How do you believe? In what ways do you serve God?" I listened to his questions, and when he was done I said, "I will answer you, but first you must answer a question for me. How many gods must we serve?" "Only one," he replied. I continued, "I believe in the living God of whom it is written in the Holy Scriptures: 'Hear, O Israel: The LORD our God is one LORD' [Dt. 6:4]. Now please tell me, which god do you worship?" He answered, "That is a stupid question. As I said before, there is only one God, the God of the Jewish people, and that is the God I worship. All the other so-called gods are nothing more than idols, and even though all the other people in the world worship these idols, the Jewish people worship the one true God." I then asked, "Are you saying that each nation of the world has its own god, the same as each nation has its own political leader?"

This man is extremely fanatical and does not trust anyone who does not agree with his radical views. What's more, he is very jealous for his beliefs. He belongs to a sect whose motto is, "Whoever is not for us is against us, and whoever is against us we must fight." It is written in Song of Solomon 8:6, "love is strong as death, jealousy is cruel as sheol." Regardless of what I said to him, he replied, "That is not the truth." Even when I showed him living proof from the Bible itself, he said, "You have no right to give explanations of the Scriptures because you are not a rabbi." To that I replied, "It is written in Matthew 7:6, 'Give not that which is holy unto the dogs, neither cast your pearls before swine.' " "From which book did you take that saying?" he asked. Instead of responding, I asked a question: "Which do you read better, Yiddish or Hebrew?" "Hebrew," he replied, and I said, "Good, because I have a Hebrew Bible here, and you can read it for yourself."

He was very interested in my Bible, but after looking at it carefully he asked, "How can you read such an unclean [non-Kosher] book? This contains the New Testament. How did this book even come into your possession?" I replied, "My friend, the New Testament is as much a part of the Bible as the Old Testament, and without the New Testament the Bible is incomplete." He was now very disturbed and asked, "Who told you the New Testament is part of the Holy Bible?" I answered, "Our own Jewish prophets wrote about Yeshua Hamashiah, the Lord Jesus Christ."

My neighbor's blood began to boil, and he cried out, "That is not true!" "Yes, it is true," I told him. "The lie is your denial of the truth. The Bible describes people just like you when it says, 'Hear ye indeed, but understand not; and see ye indeed, but perceive not' [Isa. 6:9]. Do you know from which book of the Bible that is taken?" "Yes, it is from the Prophet Isaiah," he replied. "Tell me about the God spoken of by Isaiah," I said. "Is he only for the Jewish people, as you said before?" I then read Isaiah 34:1: "Come near, ye nations, to hear; and hearken, ye peoples: let the earth hear, and all that is therein; the world, and all things that come forth from it." I then said, "You can see from this passage that there is only one God, and he is for all the nations of the world. He has provided salvation through His Son, the Lord Jesus Christ, for the Jewish people as well as all the other people of the world. He did this because He loves us; He loves all mankind. But, as it is written in Isaiah 1:3, 'The ox knoweth his owner, and the ass, his master's crib, but Israel doth not know; my people doth not consider.' "

He was very quiet for a while and then said, "I must leave now, but I will return and continue this conversation." I assured him that he would be welcome in my home any time.

I pray that the Lord will cause this man to search the Scriptures and question the validity of his own beliefs. I trust I will have more open doors to witness to him about the God who shed His own blood for the sins of all people of the world, Jewish and Gentile alike, and who will receive anyone who calls on Him in true faith.

—1989

## ZVI AND HIS WIFE
## ARE MIRACULOUSLY SPARED

Miracles do not happen every day; therefore, when they do occur, we must thank the Lord, who alone has the power to perform miracles. So it was with my wife and me on Thursday, July 6. We had gone from our home in Jerusalem to Tel Aviv on an errand. When we finished our business, my wife looked at her watch and said, "It's almost time to catch the bus back to Jerusalem. We'd better get to the bus station because I want to get home early." I, on the other hand, was in no hurry. "Why do we have to rush home?" I asked. "We don't have any babies waiting for us. Let's take our time." In the end, of course, I gave in and we hurried along.

When we arrived at the bus station, we learned that we had just missed the bus to Jerusalem. My wife was a bit upset and said, "You see, I told you we were going to miss our bus!" I tried to calm her and said, "Don't worry, the next bus will come along soon." Sure enough, 15 minutes later the next bus arrived, and we were on our way home.

About a half hour after leaving Tel Aviv, we heard the dreadful news. The bus that had left Tel Aviv before ours—the one my wife and I were hurrying to catch—had been attacked by a PLO terrorist at Abu Ghosh. He caused the driver to lose control, and the bus careened off the road and came to rest at the bottom of a hill. Fourteen people were killed, and many more were seriously injured. (A 15th person died in the hospital a few weeks later.) As we passed the site of the crash, we could see ambulances and helicopters coming and going, taking the injured to hospitals.

Of course, everyone on our bus was outraged about this attack, but we realized there was nothing we could do to bring those people back to life. Unfortunately, at times like this the spiritual blindness of the Israeli people becomes very apparent. Upon hearing of the accident, the man sitting in front of us said, "The minute I get home I am going to spread pure oil on the mezuzah [small case containing Scripture] on my doorpost. We all must do this. In that way we will honor God and thank Him for preserving our lives."

I was surprised at his concept of how to thank God, but I realized I must go slowly in responding because of the shock of the situation. I said, "I'm not sure that is the right thing to do at a time like this." He became very apprehensive and said, "You do not have a Yiddish heart." I replied, "I will not rush home and spread pure oil on the mezuzah because it will do nothing for me or for those poor people who were killed and injured. Such superstitions cannot comfort anyone. I am even now praying for the injured, that the Lord will heal them, and for the families of the dead, that the Lord will comfort them at this time of great loss. As for the dead, I can only hope they had a right relationship with God. If so, I know they are in heaven."

We had to drive far out of our way because many roads were closed due to the accident. The longer we traveled around the accident scene, the more foolish this man's statements became, and I sensed that many of the other people on the bus were agitated with this one who considered himself so religious. He, of course, was equally unhappy that no one would agree with him. I finally began to speak with him about his spiritual condition. I said, "You feel that you are right with God, but you are very far from having a proper relationship with Him. You are spiritually blind, and, as it is written, 'if the blind lead the blind, both shall fall into the ditch' [Mt. 15:14]."

This statement caught the attention of some of the passengers who were from Oriental cultures and held strange religious practices, including "evil eyes," and they became upset with me. But even they agreed that this man was speaking foolishly. I said, "Oh, that someone would remove the dust from your eyes." This statement made him extremely angry, and he replied, "That is enough! I do not want to hear anymore from you. I do not even believe that you are Jewish!" I assured him that I was a Jew, but he responded, "No! You are not! You talk just like the Gentiles, and I am sure you are one of them." Some of the other passengers agreed, and they began to be suspicious of me. But we still had a long way to go before reaching Jerusalem, and I was able to tell them about myself—about my love for Israel, my participation in the wars to save this nation from our Arab enemies, and my children, who all have served their country with pride and distinction. I then challenged the man to prove that he was a better Jew than I.

But, of course, this was not a competition about who had done more for his country. I was eager to show him, and all the others who were listening, how to worship the God of Israel in true faith rather than through the superstitions and false beliefs that have been passed down by mere men through the centuries. I said, "We, as the Chosen People of God, should be a light to all the nations of the world. But how can we go to the other nations and say, 'If you spread pure oil on your doorpost, you will be cleansed from your sins and find acceptance with God'? That is ridiculous, and the nations would think we were fools if we tried to convince them of such nonsense.

"Please, think for yourselves," I urged the others around me. "Do not follow the empty faith of false teachers. God told our forefathers in Deuteronomy 6:14, 'Ye shall not go after other gods, of the gods of the people who are round about you.' Everything I have told you is written in our own Hebrew Scriptures. If you open your eyes and read God's Word, rather than the many books of tradition, you will see for yourselves what the Lord has done for us, what He expects from us, and how He wants us to worship Him. As it is written, 'For thou art an holy people unto the LORD thy God; the LORD thy God hath chosen thee to be a special people unto himself, above all people who are upon the face of the earth' [Dt. 7:6]. God loves us and wants us to be the 'special people' He intended us to be." For the remainder of the ride, we had a good discussion about the Lord and how to worship Him according to His will.

As we arrived home that evening, my wife and I agreed that it had been an unforgettable day. We praised the Lord for miraculously preserving our lives by delaying our arrival at the bus station by just a few short minutes. We prayed fervently for those who were injured in the tragedy, for their loved ones, and for the families of those who were killed. We prayed for the PLO terrorist who had caused this disaster, and for others like him. They need to know the Lord Jesus as their Savior and understand God's perfect will for them and for their bitter enemies, the Israelis. We also prayed for the man on the bus who was so confused about how to approach a holy, righteous God and properly thank Him for saving his physical life. Finally, we prayed that he and the other passengers on the bus will seek the Lord and allow Him to save their spiritual lives as He did their physical lives.

—1989

# NO ONE WILL REMEMBER HER

It is no secret that people fear death. It is an unknown commodity, and people are naturally afraid of the unknown. But death cannot be avoided. As it is written in Ecclesiastes 12:7, "Then shall the dust return to the earth as it was, and the spirit shall return unto God, who gave it." God has given each of us an eternal spirit, and because the Lord gave Himself for us on the cross, all people who believe in Him will live with Him eternally, even after their physical bodies die.

Recently an elderly woman in my neighborhood died, and because she lived alone, she was dead for four days before her body was discovered. When the police finally came to remove the body, many of her neighbors, including myself, gathered around and spoke quietly to one another. As we were talking, one of this woman's relatives, who lived nearby, began to talk to me. He said, "I am sorry that this dear old lady has died, and it is even sadder because she has no children to take care of her in death. My wife and I have no children, so we have already purchased our graves and taken care of our own funeral arrangements. Most importantly, we have given a large sum of money to the synagogue to guarantee that someone will say *kaddish* [*prayer for the dead*] when we die and light a *yahrzeit lamp* [*memorial candle*] each year on the anniversary of our deaths. Of course, we could do all this because we have the money, but what will happen to this poor old lady? She had no money, no children, and now that she is dead she is like a stone dropped into the sea—no one will remember her ever again."

I was saddened by this man's remarks and said, "It is possible that this poor old lady will some day be richer than you." "How can that be? She is dead, never to live again," he responded. I told him, "If she had a proper relationship with God through His Son, she will be rich in eternity." I then related the account of the rich man and the beggar from Luke 16:19-23, specifically pointing out verse 22: "And it came to pass that the beggar died, and was carried by the angels into Abraham's bosom; the rich man also died, and was buried."

These people were surprised to hear this story and asked how I had come to this conclusion. I replied, "This is not my own personal conclusion; it is written in the Bible. King David did not fear what would happen to his physical body. Instead, he prayed, 'take not thy holy Spirit from me' [Ps. 51:11]. The beloved 23rd Psalm was not written for the rich only, but for everyone who trusts in the Lord and 'will dwell in the house of the LORD forever' [v. 6]." The man then asked, "Don't you ever think about what will happen to you when you die?" I answered, "My future is secure because I have received the Lord as my Savior, and in Him there is no death or darkness, only life and light."

It was obvious that these people did not understand what I meant. They had immigrated to Israel from Russia, where they knew nothing about God, and since coming to Israel they have listened only to the stories of the old rabbis told in the synagogues. I asked if they had ever read the Bible, and the man replied, "How could we read the Bible in Russia? It was impossible! And even if we could have gotten a Bible and read it, we wouldn't have understood it because the Bible is written in Hebrew, which we did not know in Russia." I said, "But you have been in Israel for several years; surely by now you know Hebrew." "Oh yes, we know it and can speak it," he replied, "but we do not understand it well enough to read something as deep as the Bible."

At times like this I am grateful that the Lord has blessed me with a knowledge of several languages. I took out my Bible and read to them, in Hebrew, John 14:19, "Because I live, ye shall live also"; Job 19:25, "I know that my redeemer liveth, and that he shall stand at the latter day upon the earth," and Isaiah 26:19, "Thy dead men shall live, together with my dead body shall they arise." I then translated these verses into Russian, so that there would be no misunderstanding on their part.

This couple could not accept the concept of resurrection and life after death. Referring to the lady who had just died, the man said, "We have all seen this dead body with our own eyes. How can you say that she will live again?" It is not easy to speak with such stiffnecked people, and I told them, "The longer you go without coming to a true faith in the Lord, the harder it will be for you to understand and accept His principles for our lives. Of course I understand that no one wants to die, but there is a way that we can be prepared to meet our God when we leave this earthly life. It is written in Ezekiel 18:4, 'the soul that sinneth, it shall die,' but the Lord has given us a free choice concerning the destiny of our souls. We can come to Him at any time during our earthly life and ask for forgiveness of our sins. He will grant our request at that very moment and give us the assurance of eternal life with Him in heaven. Or, we can reject His love for us, but then we will die in our sins and spend eternity in the Lake of Fire, forever separated from God."

I have often found that it is easier to speak about God with an Ultra-Orthodox Jew than it is to speak with someone who has never read the Bible and has no knowledge of God and His love for us. But, as the Lord said, we must all begin as little children and take that first step, and then another step, and another. I thank the Lord that He has given me the strength to accept the verbal abuse that usually comes from an experience such as this, as well as the patience to continue explaining spiritual things to anyone who is willing to listen.

The Lord said, "Whosoever, therefore, shall humble himself as this little child, the same is greatest in the kingdom of heaven" (Mt. 18:4). These words gave me much courage, and I was able to continue my conversation with this couple. When we parted, they were no longer hurling accusations at me but were friendly and thanked me for spending time with them. And I knew I had done what the Lord expected of me—sown the seed. I pray that God will water that seed and eventually grant the harvest of these souls to eternal life as they think about the things I shared with them and give serious consideration to their eternal destiny. There are many Russian émigrés in Israel these days, and I pray that the Lord will give me and other believers opportunities to speak with them. Perhaps they will open their hearts to the God they have so long denied.

—1990

## A LITTLE DOG PAVES THE WAY

The Lord Jesus said, "when they bring you unto the synagogues…be not anxious how or what thing ye shall answer, or what ye shall say; For the Holy Spirit shall teach you in the same hour what ye ought to say" (Lk. 12:11-12). I praise God that I have this truth to strengthen me as I witness for Him in the land of Israel.

I believe it is healthy to have a good laugh occasionally, and so it was on a pleasant Sabbath day recently. My son and his family had gone out for the day, and they left their small dog with my wife and me to *pet-sit*. Shortly after they left, I realized it was time to take the dog out for a walk, and it was just at the hour when people were returning home from the Sabbath prayer services at the synagogues. I live near a synagogue, and as I was walking the dog, an Orthodox family with many children approached me. The children were delighted to see the dog and started to play with him, and their father was happy to see them having such a good time.

I doubt that this man expected what happened next. As he watched his children frolicking on the ground around his feet, the little dog occupied himself by chewing on the tassels of the man's prayer scarf. Of course, I did not notice what the dog was doing or I would have stopped him, but there is an old saying, *When milk is spilled, you cannot bring it back to the pot.* While I had a good laugh about the situation, the man was not amused, and his joy in watching his children quickly turned to dismay and anger. He looked at me with hatred in his eyes and said, "Look what has happened. From one side I made a great *mitzvah* [*good deed*] by allowing my children to enjoy themselves, but from the other side I have made a great sin by allowing your unclean dog to defile my beautiful long tassels. He ate my most holy possession. I kiss these tassels three times a day, and now they are no longer holy."

I responded, "Your tassels were never holy, and they never will be. If you know the Jewish Scriptures, you should be aware that the tradition of having tassels on the prayer scarf is taken from Numbers 15:37-41, where the Lord commanded the Israelites to place fringes and a blue cord on the hems of their garments. They were to serve as a visual reminder of the Lord's commandments to them, but God never said they were holy. Apparently you have never known the real significance of the tassels that you and many generations before you have placed over your eyes and kissed every day. There are many men who would never be separated from their tassels but who are sitting in prison today. There is certainly nothing holy about them. Furthermore, the Lord never meant for you to place the tassels over your eyes. Rather, He wants you to look at them as they hang on your garment and thereby remember what He expects of you."

The man said, "Now you have gone too far. How do you know what the Lord expects of me?" I replied, "I know exactly what He expects of you. He wants you to keep his commandments. Also, as it is written in Joel 2:13, 'tear your heart, and not your garments, and turn unto the LORD, your God.' Your tassels are more important to you than your faith in the Lord, but you can see from this verse that your faith in Him is more important to God than your tassels. Tomorrow I will be happy to go with you to a store and purchase more tassels for your prayer scarf, so that people can see how holy you are on the outside, but that will not affect the attitude of your heart toward God."

At that point he asked his wife to take the children home. This stiff-necked man had become extremely agitated and said, "As a Jew, you should know that it is our obligation to wear tassels on our garments as long as we live." I replied, "Wearing tassels is not as important as receiving the Lord as your Savior. And this is not accomplished by practicing superstitions through which you believe you are keeping the commandments of the Lord. What is the point of keeping His commandments if you do not understand why you are doing it?"

This made him furious, but in time he became calm and eventually said, "Now I know with whom I should be spending time. It will be a great privilege for me to stop in and see you on my way home from the synagogue. Perhaps I will be able to bring a lost soul back to God." I was not surprised at his statement, and I let him go on for a while. Then his attitude changed abruptly—he apparently recognized himself for who he was and sensed the irony in someone like himself trying to bring another person back to God. He told me he had come to Israel from New York, where he had been a drug addict. He admitted that he was ashamed of his past but said he had repented.

I then whispered a silent prayer and forged ahead as tactfully as possible. I said, "You thought you had repented when you began to dress in black clothes and wear side curls and a beard, but those outward signs will not help you. They are good on only one day of the year, Purim—carnival time! You must open your heart before the Lord and ask for His forgiveness of your sins." I thought this statement would make him angry, but instead he asked in whom I placed my faith and how I had come to believe as I do.  For the next hour, I had the great privilege of telling this Orthodox Jewish man how I had found Jesus, my Messiah and Savior.  I could see that at times he was a little suspicious, but he was courteous.  At the end of our long conversation, we had a friendly and gracious parting.

Who would have thought that a little dog could pave the way for such a serious discussion and an opportunity to explain to this man that faith in God is more important than the tassels he has held so dear through the years?  This could only have been the work of the living God, and I am now praying that He will give me further opportunities with this man.  Perhaps some day he will discard his beloved tassels and tear his heart, not his garments.

—1990

## SO LONG OUR HOPES ARE NOT YET LOST

In Deuteronomy 20:1 it is written, "be not afraid…for the LORD thy God is with thee." Here in Israel, we are living in the light of this promise day by day as we face SCUD missile attacks from Iraq. We are sure of His divine protection; therefore, we can sing confidently the words of our national anthem, Hatikva: *"Od lo av-da tik va-te-nu"* (*So long our hopes are not yet lost*). We also believe that where there is life, there is hope, and that is especially true at this time. Even with missiles being dropped on us nightly, people are going about their daily routines with high morale because they know that God has said, "I have set watchmen upon thy walls, O Jerusalem, who shall never hold their peace day nor night" (Isa. 62:6). Although the vast majority of our people do not believe in the Messiah, they do know and trust in the promises of God to His Chosen People of Israel.

There are, however, many new immigrants in Israel, particularly those from the Soviet Union, who do not know the promises of God. They have lived all their lives under the red flag of communism, and when they arrived in Israel, it was like coming to another planet. They must start their lives over, and that means learning about God. As soon as they arrive, they are contacted by Ultra-Orthodox elements, whose job it is to bring them into the fold of Judaism. They have free access to the émigrés, but the émigrés are told not to have any contact with people who believe in Christ. Although the Orthodox are trying to brainwash the Soviet Jews with their false doctrines, they will not succeed because truth conquers all. And when are people most interested in learning the truth? In times of trouble, such as Israel is experiencing now.

I consider it an obligation to go to such people and comfort them with the Word of God, and I am thankful that the Lord has given me the ability to speak their language. When I first engage in a conversation with a new immigrant, it is not with warnings but in the spirit of friendship. Then, when I have gained his trust, we can be open with each other and free to say what is on our minds. In this way, I guide him as he takes those first steps on the road to true knowledge of God through faith in our Savior, the Lord Jesus Christ.

Initially, the émigrés are surprised to learn that a Jewish person would believe in Christ, especially in Israel. Even as missiles are raining down on their heads, they seem more interested in knowing how and why a Jewish person can believe in Jesus. One émigré told me, "It is impossible for a Jew to praise the name of this one whom Jews have hated through the centuries." I replied, "I have heard many people say this. You may also think that a Jewish person who believes in Christ hates Israel and anything that pertains to this nation. That is not true, but it is not your fault if you believe it. You have been brainwashed against believers from the moment you stepped off the plane. I have not come to tell you stories, such as those in the many commentaries of the rabbis. That is all you will hear from your Orthodox friends, but, as a true child of God and a good citizen of Israel, it is my duty to show you the right way to approach God, as it is explained in the Holy Bible.  If you read the Jewish Scriptures for yourself, you will understand how to have true faith in God.  You can see that I do not have with me any of the old commentary books—no stories, no traditions.  But, if you want it—and only if you want it—I will give you a Bible in the Russian language.  After reading it, you can make your own decision about God."

Even though the immigrants have been instructed to stay away from believers, they are very independent and want to make their own decisions in their new land, and they are open to discussion.  Of course, some are skeptical because of the warnings they have received.  Some of the émigrés asked me if believers in the Lord are against the Jewish religion.  I responded, "I am not against any religion if it is in accordance with the Holy Bible.  As it is written in Deuteronomy 12:32, 'Whatsoever thing I command you, observe to do it; thou shalt not add thereto, nor diminish from it.'  But, I am sorry to say, most of the people of Israel are far from being the 'holy people unto the LORD thy God' that He has instructed them to be in Deuteronomy 7:6.  And, they are the very people who are telling you how to worship God.  I am not trying to give you orders; I only want to help you find the Lord, your Savior.  Then you will truly be His Chosen People."

These immigrants were very moved by our conversation.  They said they had learned more in one hour than they did during several days of instruction from their assigned "guides."  I pray that the Lord will give me more opportunities to speak with Soviet immigrants.  I am also praying that as they read the Scriptures, the Lord alone will be their Guide and lead them into His truth, which alone will make them free (Jn. 8:32).  Finally, during these difficult days, I "Pray for the peace of Jerusalem; they shall prosper who love thee" (Ps. 122:6).

—1991

# WISDOM WITHOUT FAITH IS USELESS

I recently noticed several posters in my neighborhood announcing that a famous rabbi would be speaking at our community center. I remembered him from many years ago, when he was a popular television entertainer, but then he "repented" and is now lauded as one of the greatest rabbis of our time. His picture and quotes often appear in Israeli newspapers. When I saw these posters, I decided that I must see this *great one* in person, rather than on television, as I had done many years before.

It was announced that he would appear at 8 p.m., but he did not arrive until 9 p.m., which I did not consider to be a good beginning. There were more than three hundred people packed into a small auditorium waiting to see their hero, and I think I was the only one who did not have his head covered, as all good Jews feel they must do. When he did not arrive as scheduled, I asked some of the men around me why such a well-known rabbi could not keep his word, but they all defended him, saying that he was very busy and we must be patient.

He finally arrived, and everyone stood up, applauding and

cheering for him.  When the commotion died down, he immediately started to speak, without so much as a "Shalom" to greet the crowd.  And what did he speak about?  The fictitious stories passed down from generation to generation—nothing new, just the same old fallacies he and many other rabbis continually relate.  He concluded by saying that the most important thing a Jew can do is study the writings of our fathers, which he stated is even more important than having faith in God!  Knowledge and the traditions of Judaism are all that count.

The three hundred people gathered in the auditorium listened to this man as if he had been sent straight from heaven.  But I was troubled by what he said.  Although I knew that the crowd would go against me if I spoke up, I had to say what was in my heart.  I silently prayed, asking the Lord to give me courage, and then I rose to my feet and said to the rabbi, "Please explain how knowledge can be more important than faith in God, when the Scriptures clearly tell us, 'the just shall live by his faith' [Hab. 2:4]." The rabbi seemed annoyed by my remark and replied, "I do not have time to answer you." I, nevertheless, continued. "Do you and other great, learned, wise ones have some kind of an insurance policy to get you into heaven?  What about our father Abraham?  He never went to a great university, but the Scriptures say, 'he believed in the LORD; and he counted it to him for righteousness' [Gen. 15:6]. Are you now declaring that Abraham's faith in God was of no value because he did not go to a great school and study all his life?  Just look at what the great, learned people of our day have done with their knowledge.  They have built atom bombs and stockpiled chemicals to kill people, and the nations of the world live in constant fear of these *brilliant* ones.  I am sure that if such people were more concerned about faith in the Lord and loving Him as He loves us, they would do more good for the world than their great knowledge has accomplished thus far."

By now the rabbi was very unhappy with me because I had diverted the attention of the crowd away from him. Almost everyone in the auditorium was looking at me, waiting to hear what I would say next. The rabbi asked me to explain what I meant. In that instant, the Lord brought to my memory the reassuring words of Luke 12:11-12: "when they bring you unto the synagogues, and unto magistrates, and powers, be not anxious how or what thing ye shall answer, or what ye shall say; For the Holy Spirit shall teach you in the same hour what ye ought to say." He also brought to my remembrance that great chapter about faith, Hebrews 11, and I shared with the audience all the things our forefathers experienced because of their great faith in God. I told them, "It is written, 'Now faith is the substance of things hoped for, the evidence of things not seen…But without faith it is impossible to please him' [Heb. 11:1, 6]."

The rabbi was growing nervous. "All these people came here to see me," he said. "The posters advertised my speech, and you have no right to take the spotlight away from me." He was upset, and with good reason. All the people who had applauded and shouted, "We have come here to listen to our great rabbi," were now very quiet, waiting to hear his response to the things I had said. No one seemed inclined to make any trouble, which only added to the rabbi's dilemma. You see, whenever he goes out to speak, he takes along several bodyguards to protect him, since his remarks often cause dissent in his audiences. But on this occasion, everyone was so quiet that even the bodyguards, who were there to see that not one hair of the rabbi's head was harmed, were listening to me instead of to their employer. The entire situation surprised me greatly, but of course I realized that it was the Lord's doing.

The rabbi said, "Since you have changed this meeting into an open discussion, explain to us how you arrived at the strange position you hold." I was grateful for this opportunity and said, "It is good to be wise, but wisdom without faith is useless, especially for a religious leader such as yourself. How can you expect to bring others to faith in God when you do not consider faith to be as important as knowledge? In fact, why would you even want to encourage people to be faithful to God, if faith is not necessary? Now I want to ask the people in the audience a question: Who do you think is greater, the wisest professor who has no faith, or a man who has spent his life out in the desert, has never attended a school, but is faithful to the Lord? Which one of these two will be blessed by God?" Most of the people responded that the one from the desert—the uneducated man who was faithful to the Lord—was more important in God's sight and would be blessed by Him.

"You are correct," I told them, "for it is written in Isaiah 40:3, 'The voice of him that crieth in the wilderness, Prepare ye the way of the LORD, make straight in the desert a highway for our God.' This voice did not come from Oxford University, but from the Judean desert, from where he cried to every heart in Israel, 'Every valley shall be exalted, and every mountain and hill shall be made low; and the crooked shall be made straight, and the rough places plain; And the glory of the LORD shall be revealed, and all flesh shall see it together' [Isa. 40:4-5]."

The rabbi was now furious with me. He said, "I came here to speak for only one hour, and you have turned it into two hours. You have wasted my valuable time, and now I must leave. I never want to see you at one of my meetings again!" And with that, he stomped off the stage.

He was obviously angry, but I was happy that these people had listened to me with such interest and patience. I would never have believed that such a thing could happen, but the Lord is able to do the impossible. I pray that the small seed that was planted in that large group will grow into a great, fruitful tree.

—1991

## THE MIRACLE OF THE SNOWSTORM

We recently experienced something we have not seen in Israel for many years—a storm that produced 16 inches of snow! The children were delighted that they had a few days off from school and could romp in the snow and build snowmen. The older people, on the other hand, were not so happy. Many had to stay at home since public transportation was almost at a standstill. The many traffic accidents resulted in downed power lines and loss of electricity, and it was difficult for repairmen to get to the senior citizens.

I live in the center of my settlement, and most people there know me. Some know me as a helpful person who will come to their homes and make various repairs without charging them. But others know me as an "apostate" and accuse me of trying to lead them away from the faith and preaching the gospel of Christ. During the snowstorm, the Lord performed a miracle by bringing to my door someone who I thought knew me only as an apostate, but apparently he was aware of my other reputation as well. I must confess that I was surprised when this well-known rabbi came to my home, not with a sour face as on the other occasions when he had visited me. No, this time he came with a pleasant expression, and in a kind voice he said, "Well, Zvi, you have won the war. I need you now! I think you can help me." I asked, "What do you need? I will do my best to be of service to you." He replied, "We have no electricity in our home. From what I have heard, I am sure that you can bring back the light." "Of course, let's go," I said, as I picked up my toolbox, which is always at the ready, just like a doctor with his black bag.

As we approached the rabbi's home, I remarked, "Now we are going into the darkness, but hopefully we will soon bring back the light to our eyes, and, more importantly, to our hearts." After only a few minutes of work, I was able to restore power to the home, and the light came on—and with it came great joy to the rabbi and his family. I then recited a verse of Scripture to the family: "The people that walked in darkness have seen a great light; they that dwell in the land of the shadow of death, upon them hath the light shined" (Isa. 9:2).

Because I was a guest in the rabbi's home, and not only a guest but someone who had performed a valuable service for him, I felt the liberty to speak about a subject I had never mentioned in his presence—faith in the Lord. In his own home! In the presence of his wife and children! And, what's more, they even invited me to sit and have a cup of tea with them as we talked. Such an opportunity comes along perhaps once in a jubilee, and I prayed within my heart that the Lord would enable me to speak in a way that was honoring to Him.

I sensed that this occasion bore fruit. Although the rabbi is far from believing in the Lord Jesus Christ, he was so grateful for what I had done that he vowed never again to speak against me or call me an apostate, telling people that I distribute poison and want them to leave the faith of their fathers. The same God who brought about the miracle of the snowfall also did a work in the rabbi's heart that had before seemed impossible. Truly, the blind can see and the deaf can hear.

As I was about to leave, the rabbi asked me what he owed for the work I had done. I replied, "There is no charge. In such situations, we must do as the Talmud says: 'In times of distress, the children of Israel must be responsible for each other's well-being.' Because I believe in God, He has put a great love in my heart for my neighbors. That is not what I say; it is written in the law of the Lord: 'thou shalt love thy neighbor as thyself: I am the LORD' [Lev. 19:18]. And you are my neighbor."

At this, the rabbi jumped up and said, "What? Do you actually believe what the Bible says?" "Yes," I replied. "As a matter of fact, the Bible is the foundation of the faith in which I believe?" Then he said, "As you know, I am a respected rabbi, and no one has ever had the courage to say such a thing to me. You have the greatest *chutzpah* [*impertinence*] I have ever seen. But now your own tongue has trapped you. Show me where it is written about this man Jesus in the Bible. Prove it to me before my entire family."

I responded, "First, I want you to know that I am happy you asked this. I am not trapped, as you believe." Then I read to him Micah 5:2: "But thou, Bethlehem Ephrathah, though thou be little among the thousands of Judah, yet out of thee shall he come forth unto me that is to be ruler in Israel, whose goings forth have been from of old, from everlasting." "Ah, yes," he replied, "but this one in whom you believe never ruled Israel. He was crucified on a cross." "You are right," I said, "and everyone stared at Him as He hung there. But you forget that it is also written in Zechariah 12:10, 'they shall look upon me whom they have pierced, and they shall mourn for him, as one mourneth for his only son, and shall be in bitterness for him, as one that is in bitterness for his firstborn.' It is also written in Ezekiel 39:29, 'Neither will I hide my face any more from them; for I have poured out my Spirit upon the house of

Israel, saith the Lord GOD.' I could go on and on, page after page, showing you where the Bible speaks about this one whom you ridicule. If you want to hear more, I can stay as long as you like."

He then quoted Jeremiah 12:1: "Why doth the way of the wicked prosper?" I asked, "Who are the wicked? Those who believe in the living God? Or those who worship a false faith and dance around the golden calf?" After this, our discussion became very heated, but also very interesting, and I was able to tell him things about the Lord that I could never have said before.

I know that this encounter will produce fruit some day. I pray that I will have further opportunities to speak to this rabbi, trusting that one day he and his family will be brought out of spiritual darkness into spiritual light, just as they were brought out of physical darkness into physical light during the snowstorm.

—1991

## A SHEEP AMONG WOLVES

In Isaiah 11:6 it is written, "The wolf also shall dwell with the lamb, and the leopard shall like down with the kid." One day recently I prayed before leaving my home to go out and witness about the Lord Jesus Christ, but I had no specific destination in mind as I boarded the bus for Jerusalem. I got off the bus in the center of the new city and began to walk down the street. As I stopped at a corner, I looked around and was surprised when I realized where I was—in front of the headquarters of the *Yad Le 'Ahim.* This group is almost like a commando team, and they fight against those of us who believe in Christ.

I stood there, just looking at the sign for a few seconds, and then I thought, *Well, here I am, and it was to places just like this that our Lord said, "Behold, I send you forth as sheep in the midst of wolves; be ye, therefore, wise as serpents, and harmless as doves"* (Mt. 10:16). This verse gave me special courage, and, without an invitation, I found myself inside the office of this anti-missionary organization. A man approached me and asked what I wanted and if he could be of help. I replied, "I saw your large sign proclaiming ʻ*Yad Le ʾAhim!* [*Hand to a Brother!*] , and so I came in to learn how you can help me, your brother.ˮ

The man was very kind and invited me to have a seat. He then explained the purpose of the organization. ʻWe extend our hands to rescue our brothers who have fallen into the trap of the apostates, people who want to poison them and capture their souls. Such people are very dangerous, and we must stand guard day and night against their heresy and apostasy. This is our holy duty! Now you know about the important service we render to God and our country.ˮ

Then it was my turn to speak. ʻI didnʼt know that people could die from the ʻpoisonʼ you mentioned. I have never read in the newspaper that someone died from reading the Bible.ˮ When they heard this, everyone in the office turned around to look at me, and the gentleman to whom I was speaking asked, in an unpleasant tone of voice, ʻHow do you know that those apostates believe in the Bible? Are you one of them?ˮ ʻI am!ˮ I replied. ʻI am one who actively serves God and my country by telling people how to come to the Lord, our Savior, and be faithful to Him according to the law rather than according to the word of commandos, who themselves are walking in the darkness and cannot find the light. They want others to follow them into the darkness, but I believe what is written in Leviticus 19:14, ʻThou shalt not…put a stumbling block before the blind.ʼ This is what you are doing—trapping the blind in darkness!ˮ

By now, all of the office staff had gathered around me, and when I finished speaking, they whispered to one another for a short time, and then the man to whom I was speaking said, ʻWe have listened very carefully to you, and we have arrived at the conclusion that you are one of those dangerous ones bringing spiritual poison to the new immigrants from Russia. You are one of the ones we are fighting so hard and about whom we warn these new citizens. How can you have the *chutzpah* to come in here and try to brainwash us also? You are insolent!ˮ

I replied, "I only want to show you that you don't have to work so hard. We are not dangerous, and we are not trying to brainwash the Russian immigrants. You go to them with your many books of commentary, but they have never heard of them or the men who wrote them, and so they are not interested in them. Why don't you do as I do—bring them the books of the law [Genesis to Deuteronomy], which God gave to the people of Israel through Moses on Mount Sinai? Even though they are not as familiar with the law as we are, having come from an atheistic society, they have heard of the law because it was passed down through many generations. Now they want to know what it says. I show them the book of books, the Bible, because in it is written everything they need to know. Through this book they can learn who their God is, who their Savior is, and how they can prepare themselves to meet Him one day."

The man could no longer listen quietly and said in a loud, agitated voice, "Do you tell them they must believe in this man Jesus? Do you tell them that by believing in Him they will be saved?" "There, you have said it yourself," I responded, "and you must know what you are talking about because it is in the Bible, which you have studied very carefully. I did not write the Bible, you know. It was written by the prophets under divine inspiration. Your saying that people can read about Jesus in the Bible is a great blessing to my heart, because I have known and believed this to be true for many years."

When I made that statement, it was as if I had ignited a big fire. "How can you say that? Aren't you ashamed?" he shouted. "No, my dear," I replied. "Stop calling me 'my dear.' We are not your *dears*," he said. I then read Isaiah 50:7, "For the Lord GOD will help me; therefore shall I not be confounded; therefore have I set my face like a flint, and I know that I shall not be ashamed." "I know in whom I have believed, and I am not ashamed," I told him.

"Do you also kneel before this man?" he asked. "Yes, of course," I replied. "Daniel knelt three times a day and prayed to God. King

David said in Psalm 95:6, 'Oh, come, let us worship and bow down; let us kneel before the LORD our maker.' Can I do any less than our great ancestors? You see, I am not like you—going to people with warnings. Instead, I go to them with the love of God. And so, again I call you 'my dear.' I know that you hate me, but I want you to know that I love you because the Lord instructed us, 'by love serve one another' [Gal. 5:13]. The most popular commandment in the law is found in Leviticus 19:18, 'thou shalt love thy neighbor as thyself.' You are my neighbor, and so I love you."

Shortly thereafter, our conversation ended, and I left these people to ponder the things I had told them. I hope to have further contact with them and pray that one day they will see the light that is found in the Lord Jesus Christ. Then we can break this endless chain of the blind leading the blind.

—1992

## IT IS POSSIBLE IF GOD WILLS IT

The Orthodox Jews have many sayings, and by using them they can turn black into white and white into black. Of course, all of this is done in a nice way so that no one is offended. I have contact with many Orthodox Jews in my neighborhood, especially older people for whom I make home repairs, and they usually invite me to their *Semahot* (family celebrations such as bar mitzvahs, weddings, and other religious observances). Although they know what I believe, and in spite of our many heated discussions about religion, they never forget me during their times of rejoicing.

So it was that a father recently invited me to his son's bar mitzvah. And what was the first thing he said when he saw me? "Good for the righteous, good for his neighbor; but woe to the righteous, woe to his neighbor!" A bar mitzvah occurs when a Jewish boy becomes 13 years of age, at which time he assumes all of the religious obligations necessary to keep the law. From that time on, the boy is responsible for himself before the Lord. I attend bar mitzvahs and other religious festivals because they provide good opportunities to witness about the Lord. Of course, it is not easy to speak about Him because people do not want to hear what I have to say, but He gives me the courage and opens the doors.

Shortly after the bar mitzvah ceremony ended, an old man approached me. He knows me very well because I have made many repairs for him, and we have spoken about my faith in Christ right in his own home. He greeted me and then asked, "How can a cat come over the sea and not be wet?" I immediately understood his meaning and replied, "It is possible if God wills it. You can read of such an incident in the Scriptures. That is what the Lord did for the people of Israel when they crossed the Red Sea and came out dry. So it was with me. I crossed a sea—literally and figuratively—and came out dry! This was the will of God, so that I might meet you and tell you about my faith in Christ. If you like, we can continue the conversation about Him that we began in your home." "That would be good," he said. "Let's take a large table, and I will gather some of my friends who will be happy to take part in our conversation."

He went away for a few minutes, and while he was gone I prayed that the Lord would be with me, as He is at all times, and be my guide as I spoke to these men. I received great courage from the Lord through that prayer, and it was good that I did because the man soon returned with several friends and what he perceived to be great power, but he did not have the power of the Holy Spirit—and I did!

The first thing he asked was, "Do you have a Bible with you?" "Yes," I replied, "and I am ready to discuss it with you, but I want you to know that I did not come to this bar mitzvah to compete with you, to see who knows more about the Bible. You see, it is not enough to *know* about the Bible. The important thing is to *believe* it. You have very little knowledge of the Bible itself because you constantly study your books of commentary, and that is sad. In many cultures, people are not taught about faith in God and are not permitted to worship Him. That is not the case here in Israel, but you have not taken advantage of your freedom. You have a right to know who your Savior is." One of the men said, "I suppose you mean your Jesus." "He is not my Savior only," I told him. "Jesus came from heaven to give Himself for the whole world. So it is written in the Bible." Then these men became very agitated and started to attack me full speed. But I was happy that the true subject of our discussion—Jesus Christ, our Savior—was out in the open and that I could freely speak about my faith in Him.

Just then another old gentleman came over to our group and asked what we were discussing. When I told him that I believe in Jesus as my Savior and the Jewish Messiah, he said, "I am sorry that we—the Chosen People of Israel, who are to be examples to the people of the world and the generations to come—are running away from that truth, which is taught in the law of Moses." He then told us that he was 84 years old, and although he was lacking in physical power, he was mighty in the power of the Lord. The other men, who had been so sure of themselves, became as weak as flies. This man spoke at great length about his faith in the Lord, and he was a great inspiration to me. I had never met him before, and when he finished speaking I extended my hand to him and said, "*Hazack-Baruh!*" (*Be strong and blessed*), the synagogue greeting for the worshiper called upon to read the law.

Meeting this dear man was just another reminder that the Lord is in every place. He told me, "I heard your conversation with those evil-hearted ones, and I received the courage to speak up about my faith in the Lord. I never did that before, and I don't know who gave me such great strength." "I know," I told him. "Your strength and courage came through the power of the Lord Himself." I then asked his name, but he replied, "It is enough that God knows who I am." I agreed, saying, "God knows every one of us." I was glad to see that the other men in the group were smiling.

I pray that the Lord will continue to strengthen this dear saint, and many others like him here in Israel, to speak out for Him. Then the prophecy will be fulfilled, "out of Zion shall go forth the law, and the word of the LORD from Jerusalem" (Isa. 2:3).

—1992

# ONLY GOD CAN SEND
# A PERSON TO PARADISE

During the recent election campaign here in Israel, various candidates and parties engaged in a battle of prestige. Of course, everyone wanted to be prime minister, but, as we say, two kings cannot wear the same crown.

It was not a clean campaign, and, in addition to the usual name-calling, there were many false declarations made by the candidates on their own behalf. One candidate in particular—a rabbi running on the ticket of an Ultra-Orthodox religious party—placed an ad in the newspapers stating, "God will judge those who do not give their votes to our political party!" A few days later, the same candidate ran another ad stating, "If you vote for our party, you will earn a place in the Garden of Eden. It will be your passport to paradise!"

These statements were very disturbing to me, and the Lord gave me the courage to go to the headquarters of this party to discuss their claims. As soon as they saw that I was not wearing a hat or a beard, they became suspicious and asked, "Who are you, and what do you want here?" I replied, "Your newspaper ad states that you have the power to send people to paradise if they vote for your party. I want to know who gave you this power and if you are sure you can fulfill what you have promised. As far as I know, God Himself is the only one who has the authority to send a person to paradise. Has He given you a *power of attorney* to act on His behalf?"

These people were sure that I was crazy, and they called over one of their "fighters" to set me straight. He was very self-assured and demanded to know why I was attacking them. I responded, "I have not come here to fight against you, but I would like to know why you are using God's name in your advertising. The Ten Commandments state, 'Thou shalt not take the name of the LORD thy God in vain; for the LORD will not hold him guiltless that taketh his name in vain' [Ex. 20:7]. Therefore, I have come to ask why you made the irrational decision to misuse His name in this dirty election campaign. In Leviticus 11:44-45, the Lord clearly states His desire for His Chosen People: 'ye shall be holy; for I am holy…I am the LORD who bringeth you up out of the land of Egypt, to be your God; ye shall therefore be holy, for I am holy.' "

By now their curiosity was aroused, and they asked what political party I represented. "I do not represent any party," I replied, "but I noted that all of your campaign ads contain the name of God, and, as a believer in God according to the Holy Scriptures, I consider your statements blasphemous. I know what the Lord expects of us as His Chosen People—I know what we can do and what we cannot do—and I could not rest until I came here and clarified for you your obligations before the Lord. If I had not come to you, I would have been guilty before Him. This is not a question of which political party is best, but of our great responsibility to God. He has instructed us to go to all nations and preach the gospel of the Lord. Instead, you are misusing His name when He has clearly told us not to do so; neither are we to give false testimony [Ex. 20:7, 16]."

The man then asked, "Do you know the Talmud?" I answered, "I try the best I can to keep the law of the Lord, but I do not follow your false beliefs." He then asked, "Do you know about the 613 oral laws?" I replied, "It is impossible to keep the Ten Commandments, so how do you expect a person to keep 613 laws?" By now he was frustrated and said, "Let's get down to the bottom line. What is your faith? In what do you believe?" I replied, "I have been waiting for you to ask that question, and thank the Lord the time has now come. I assure you that no one sent me to you; I came on my own. I am sure that your bold claims and intimidating statements have kept others from confronting you before and telling you to stop these tactics. Well, I am here to do just that! And the only reason I am here is because I believe in the Lord—not according to your false traditions, but according to the Scriptures. Now you are trying to draw others into your trap, and it is my duty, before God, to try and stop you. I did not come here to threaten you, as your rabbi has done by telling people that if they do not vote for your party, God will judge them."

The man then changed the subject and asked what I thought about the coming of the Messiah, which was a major theme of that party's election campaign. I opened my Bible, read Isaiah 53, and asked, "Do you think we should be looking for the Messiah to *come*, or to *return*?" "What do you think?" he asked in return, and I replied, "I don't have to think. I know because it is written right here in the Bible, which was inspired by the Holy Spirit. I have no right to add or detract one word from this book. It is clear from the Scriptures that the Messiah has already come once and that one day soon He will come again. As you pray on Yom Kippur, 'Forever, O

LORD, thy word is settled in heaven' [Ps. 119:89]."

Before I left, they gave me the opportunity to give my testimony and tell them how I came to believe in the Lord Jesus as my Savior and Israel's Messiah.  Of course, everything I told them was backed up by Scripture.  I pray that I will have further opportunities to speak with these people and that they will see the danger of taking the Lord's name in vain.

—1992

# ALL THAT GLITTERS IS NOT GOLD!

The Lord has taught us in His Holy Word how to pray, but sometimes we repeat those words without paying attention to them. If we consider the words carefully, we can see the great meaning and value of the Lord's Prayer for our daily lives. For example, He taught us to pray, "lead us not into temptation, but deliver us from evil" (Mt. 6:13; Lk. 11:4).

The importance of that phrase was brought home to me recently when I went to the Ministry of the Interior to renew my identification card. This office also issues passports, and it is always very busy. If you want to get quick service, you must arrive at about 6 a.m., two hours before it opens. On this particular morning, I was running late and did not arrive there until 9 a.m. Naturally, the office was extremely crowded, and I thought to myself, *This is hopeless!* Nevertheless, I decided that since I was there, I would just be patient, no matter how long it took. I found an empty spot on one of the long benches and sat down to wait my turn. I immediately realized that there was something on the spot where I was sitting, and when I reached down I found a paper bag. Imagine my surprise when I looked inside and found money—a lot of money—U.S. dollars and Israeli shekels. I thought, *If I give this to the security officer, he will thank me and keep it for himself.* After all, things like this probably happen all the time. But then I remembered those words: "lead us not into temptation, but deliver us from evil."

I decided to take the money to the police station. They were happy I had brought it to them, and they gave me a receipt for it. Then one of the officers remarked "I can see by your clothes that you are not a religious person, so why did you turn in this bag of money? It is a sizable amount; surely you could have put it to good use." I replied, "All that glitters is not gold. And why do you judge people by the clothes they wear? As a police officer, you must have had many experiences with people who were well-dressed but who are now behind bars. I read in the newspaper a few weeks ago that you put one of the well-known rabbis in prison, and surely he was dressed as one who is, as you say, 'religious.' "

The officer persisted, "It is not often that we see a non-religious person like you who is so honest. I still don't understand why you brought this money to us." I responded, "It may come as a shock to you, but I do believe in the Lord, and it is because I believe in Him, and not in mammon, that I am here today. You see, if a person believes in the Lord with all his heart, money has no power over his life." I then remembered the hymn that says, "Nor silver nor gold hath obtained my redemption," and I recited the words to the officer in Hebrew. Then I asked him, "If I, as one who believes in God and am faithful to Him and His Word, were to keep this money, where is my faith? And whom should I worship, God or mammon?"

By now, our conversation had attracted the attention of several other officers who joined the discussion. Of course, they too wanted to know about me because it was hard for them to accept the fact that a man who did not have his head covered would speak about faith; however, this is nothing new in Israel. Anyone who speaks about the Lord but is not dressed like the Ultra-Orthodox is suspected of being a missionary—a word that has a bad connotation in this country. But this does not make me afraid, and I asked these officers if they knew the meaning of the word *missionary.* One replied, "It is someone who spreads a false faith." Then I asked, "What about Abraham and Jonah? Did they try to spread a false faith? Or Ezra and Nehemiah? Did they try to deceive people about God? Of course not! And yet they were all missionaries because they spoke to people about faith in the God of Israel. As a matter of fact, Jonah was punished when he disobeyed God's command to preach to the people of Nineveh."

In that police station, sitting in the midst of many officers, I was able to show clearly why I had come to them with the bag of money. I told them, "I am not like those great 'faithful' rabbis who are now in prison because they were faithful to mammon rather than to God. Where is their great faith now? And why, strictly because of the way they dress, do you consider them so holy when, in fact, they have broken the laws of God and man? It is written, 'The righteous shall flourish like the palm tree; he shall grow like a cedar in Lebanon' [Ps. 92:12]."

After a lengthy discussion, one of the officers said, "Let's get to the root of this situation. How did you come to the conclusion that your faith is right?" I told him, "I have not come to any conclusions. Rather, what I have said is from the Holy Bible, and I believe everything that is written there—nothing more, nothing less. Because of my faith, I believe in the living God rather than in mammon, and I know in my heart that it is right. It is for this reason that we are having this discussion. It is certainly not because of my wonderful personality or anything else about me. I believe in the Lord—it's that simple—and He is the one who taught us not to be blind and go after bribes or give in to temptation."

To my surprise, the officers invited me to have a cup of tea with them, and they asked me to start from the beginning and tell them about myself. I related some of my experiences in Europe during the Holocaust and told them of my 44 years here in Israel, including my long military service. And I was pleased to be able to report that throughout those 44 years, I have never had one problem with the police, which made them very happy. I thank the Lord that because of my faith in Him, rather than in mammon, I had the wonderful opportunity to witness in such an unlikely place as a police station. I pray that these officers will consider the things I told them and come to faith in Jesus as their Messiah and Savior.

—1993

# A FRUITFUL DAY

For many years, the people of Israel have been singing about the time of the Messiah's coming. Of course, we who believe in Christ according to the Scriptures know that He has already come, and so we look for His return. But not many Israelis are aware of this truth. That is why I try to tell as many people as possible about the Lord, and that is why I go to the Wailing Wall in Jerusalem every Monday and Thursday. Those are days of great celebration, as 13-year-old boys have their bar mitzvahs and assume all of the adult religious obligations of the law, a ritual that has been handed down from generation to generation.

One recent Monday, as I was preparing to go to the Wailing Wall to take part in the celebration, I decided to give something to the boys as a remembrance of this special day in their lives. I knew that each boy would receive a prayer book from his parents or friends, but there is not even a hint of the divine presence in that prayer book. Just as those young boys take upon themselves the obligation to observe the law, so I have taken upon myself the obligation to bring the Word of the Lord to those who want to truly keep His law. And so, on that Monday morning, I took with me some Bibles, all of them containing the New Testament as well as the Old Testament. Before leaving home to fulfill my obligation before the Lord, I prayed, asking Him to guide me and give me the words to say. In Israel, you must go slowly and carefully when you approach people with the Word.

When I arrived at the Wailing Wall, among the young boys celebrating their bar mitzvahs were a few Ethiopians. They were not new immigrants; they had been in Israel for several years and could speak Hebrew well. After the ceremony, I approached them and said, "I want to give each of you a gift in honor of your bar mitzvah. It is something I am sure you have not received before." Of course, they were curious and wanted to know what it was, and I gave each of them a full Bible. At first they were afraid to accept them, but I began to speak to them and explained, "There is a big difference between these Bibles and the prayer books you have received with such great joy from your parents and friends. Your prayer books were written by men—great rabbis, to be sure—but, nevertheless, just men. The Bible was written through the inspiration of the Holy Spirit of God."

Soon several other young boys joined the group, and they were very interested in what I was saying. Eventually one of their fathers came over, and he too was quite open. We spoke for a long time, and then he said to his son, "I think this is a very nice gift. Please accept it and read it." This gave me great joy and more courage. There were many people gathered around us, and they all wanted to talk about the Lord. Most of them had never heard that Jesus is the Messiah of Israel and their Savior. What a wonderful opportunity I had to tell them about Him.

After a while, an Ultra-Orthodox man approached us, and he was carrying a large *shofar* (*ram's horn*). I asked, "Why have you brought a shofar with you today? It is not a holiday." He said, "You are right." I then told him, "The Scriptures say that the shofar is symbolic of announcing the salvation of the Lord," to which he replied, "When the Messiah comes, I will blow this shofar." I opened my Bible and read Isaiah 53:5-6: "He was wounded for our transgressions, he was bruised for our iniquities; the chastisement for our peace was upon him, and with his stripes we are healed. All we like sheep have gone astray; we have turned every one to his own way, and the LORD hath laid on him the iniquity of us all." I then said, "You can see from this passage that the Messiah has already come, and someday He will come again."

The man was very interested and took the Bible from me, reading for himself the remainder of this *forbidden* chapter. All of a sudden, his countenance changed. He began to smile and was full of joy, saying, "Now is the time to announce the salvation of the Lord. Yes, I see, He has come, and now He must come back!" Then he began to blow the shofar loudly. Many people heard his trumpeting and came over to see what was happening. They could all see the great joy on his face.

Of all the times I have gone to the Wailing Wall and witnessed for the Lord, I have never seen such a reaction. As the voice of that shofar sounded in my ears, all I could think of were the words of Isaiah 40:3: "The voice of him that crieth in the wilderness, Prepare ye the way of the LORD, make straight in the desert a highway for our God."

Because the area surrounding the Wailing Wall is small, the sound of the shofar came to the ears of some rabbis, and one of them came over and asked me what I was "selling" to these "unsuspecting people." He was not glad like the others, and so I told him, "Ye have sold yourselves for nothing, and ye shall be redeemed without money." He did not like that remark and asked, "Who told you that?" I replied, "It is from our own Hebrew Scriptures—Isaiah 52:3. It was spoken by none other than the sovereign Lord Himself."

Because the Ultra-Orthodox people are suspicious of everyone, they don't believe anything unless they see it for themselves, in black and white. Of course, the rabbi did not accept anything I said as the truth, and so I showed him the verse in my Bible, along with a few other passages, including Psalm 119:89: "Forever, O LORD, thy word is settled in heaven." Eventually the rabbi realized that I believe in Christ, and he asked to see my Bible. I gave it to him and continued to point out portions in the Old Testament. But he quickly turned to the back and, upon seeing the New Testament, asked, "Do you think this belongs in our Holy Bible?" "Yes," I replied, and, to my amazement, he seemed very interested and began to look through it. Finally, he put the Bible in his pocket and, without saying another word, walked away.

What a wonderful day! As I look back, I think of the Ethiopian boys who were celebrating their passage into manhood and the accompanying obligations. I pray that they will read the Bibles I gave them and come to faith in the Lord Jesus. I think of the Ultra-Orthodox man who joyfully blew his shofar, announcing the salvation of the Lord. I pray that he will understand the things I told him and surrender his life to the Lord. I think of the rabbi who was so antagonistic but who, in the end, left with a Bible—including the New Testament—tucked into his pocket. I pray that he will read it and that his long-blinded eyes will be opened to the light of the Messiah. Finally, I pray that I will have many more fruitful days like this in the service of the Lord Jesus in His Holy City.

—1993

## AROUND THE CORNER

In Isaiah 2:3 it is written, "out of Zion shall go forth the law, and the word of the LORD from Jerusalem." Most people in Israel know this passage of Scripture, and it has been made into a song that people sing with great joy, but the Israelis do not obey the command of this verse to spread the true Word of the Lord.

One recent morning, I went to a market in Jerusalem (it is really a series of small stores where people go to look for bargains), and I saw a long line of people in front of one of the stores. Of course, I was curious to know why such a large crowd had gathered, so I asked several people what was being sold there, but no one would say. Finally, one of the sellers came along, and I asked, "What are you selling here?" He looked around cautiously for a moment and then motioned me to follow him around the corner. When we were alone, he said quietly, "A great righteous man is coming to that store soon. He can help people solve their problems, and he has performed many miracles." I asked, "How much do you have to pay for such a miracle?" and he replied, "Not much—only 280 shekels [approximately 77 U.S. dollars]."

I then asked, "Who gave him the power to do the work of the devil?" The man was surprised at my question, and I could tell that he was afraid I would talk to those standing in line to meet the great righteous man. It was obvious that the situation was making him nervous, and suddenly he dashed off, shouting as he went, "Wait here for a minute. I'll be back!" I suspected that he was going to get reinforcements, and I was right. He returned shortly with two more men, and they seemed very confident of themselves. One of them fired off a series of questions: "What do you want here? What is your business in this area? Why do you care what is happening around the corner?"

"If I walk away and do nothing," I told him, "I will be guilty of taking part in this dirty business. It is written in Ezekiel 33:7-8, 'O son of man, I have set thee a watchman unto the house of Israel…if thou dost not speak to warn the wicked from his way, that wicked man shall die in his iniquity, but his blood will I require at thine hand.' This is my obligation before God and man. Furthermore, it is written in Leviticus 26:1, 'Ye shall make no idols nor carved image, neither rear you up a standing image, neither shall ye set up any image of stone in your land, to bow down unto it: for I am the LORD your God.' The Lord has promised blessings to those who obey His Word and curses to those who disobey it. Think about it. Which do you want? You can see that everything I have said is taken from the Bible, which was written under the inspiration of the Holy Spirit of God. It is eternal, and no one can add or subtract anything from this holy book—not even one letter."

After a long discussion, one of the men asked, "Just what is it that you want? Do you want us to close this place and send all these people home on your orders?" "No, my friend," I replied. "I have read to you the orders of God Himself. I am just His insignificant servant, but I do the best I can to warn people to turn from their wicked ways." I then read to them the continuation of the command in

Ezekiel: "Nevertheless, if thou warn the wicked of his way to turn from it, if he do not turn from his way, he shall die in his iniquity, but thou hast delivered thy soul" (Ezek. 33:9). They appeared to be listening very carefully, but I could tell they were also wondering how to get me away from that place, and soon they found a way. "Because you are reading from the Bible, we know who you are," they announced. "You are a Christian, and if you do not leave this place quietly, things will not go well for you!"

I was not afraid of them, and against their warning I went around the corner and started to speak to the poor people who were waiting in line like lambs about to be led to the slaughter. I began very slowly, telling them about false teachers, and I read Jeremiah 23:25: "I have heard what the prophets said, who prophesy lies in my name, saying, I have dreamed, I have dreamed." "You must realize who this 'great righteous man' is," I told them. "He is prophesying lies in God's name. If you accept his false teaching, you will not only have to pay with your hard-earned money, you will also pay with your lives and your souls. I have come to warn you about the consequences of following such people, and I want to read to you a good example of a situation such as this found in the New Testament." I then read Matthew 7:15: "Beware of false prophets, who come to you in sheep's clothing, but inwardly they are ravening wolves." I said, "It is because I love you that I am warning you of this great danger. Think about it."

By this time, there was nothing the organizers of the meeting could do to stop me because I was in the midst of a large crowd of people who were very interested in the conversation. Some said they were there because they had many troubles, and I told them, "We are not living in a paradise on this earth, and we never will; however, the Lord is preparing a paradise for us when we leave this earth. But we will never get there by asking wicked people, like the one coming here today, to bless us. To get into God's paradise, we must come to Him in the way He has prescribed in His Holy Word. God alone can give us true blessings and solutions to our most difficult problems. Be careful that you are not bewitched by false prophets who proclaim themselves to be great righteous ones."

Naturally, some of the people in the group were uncertain about me and suggested that we go around the corner to continue our discussion. No doubt they suspected that I was a Christian. Of course, by now I knew the meaning of going "around the corner." They wanted to keep me away from the others. One man asked, "Are you a Jew?" and I replied, "I am, but we have only one God, and He does not care about nationalities. He is concerned with people's hearts and worship. I am not trying to hide anything or represent myself as something other than what I am. I believe in the Lord Jesus as my Messiah and Savior, and therefore I have to warn you against following false teachers, like the one you are waiting to see at this very moment."

Many of these people accepted my witness graciously, and some even left the line to speak further with me about the Lord. Of course, I made sure they received the right information about Him, rather than what the rabbis tell them. At the end of our conversation, I gave them New Testaments so that they could read about Him for themselves. I pray that these people will recall our conversation, read the New Testament, and come to a knowledge of the truth. Then they will have no need to seek out false teachers to help solve their problems because they will be able to take everything to the Lord, "who is able to do exceedingly abundantly above all that we ask or think" (Eph. 3:20).

—1993

# MOURNING THE CHILDREN OF MY YOUTH

I often go to Mea Shearim, the Ultra-Orthodox section of Jerusalem, because I know how deeply into sin these people have fallen, and the Word of God has charged me to warn them to come to God before it is too late.

Recently I was walking along the street in that area when I heard the voices of children singing a very old song, a song I had not heard in more than 50 years. The singing was coming from a group of students in a religious elementary school. Hearing that song, my thoughts strayed back to 1938 and the children with whom I sang it in Warsaw. Most of them are no longer alive—they perished in the Nazi death camps during the Holocaust. Yet the voices of these children sounded the same, the melody was the same, the words were the same, and the voice of the rabbi singing along with them was the same—it was as if nothing had changed.

As I stood on the street listening, I mourned for the children of my youth. They could be grandparents now, just as I am, but they are all gone, and there are very few of us left who even remember them.  I also felt great sorrow for the children who were singing now because it is such a woeful song.  The words are taken from Psalm 44:23-24:  "Awake, why sleepest thou, O Lord?  Arise, cast us not off forever.  Wherefore hidest thou thy face, and forgettest our affliction and our oppression?"  Jewish children through the centuries have been taught to sing this song with a special feeling of lament, and the more I listened, the less peace I felt in my heart.

Finally, I ventured into the school to speak with the rabbi.  When I entered, the children stopped singing and stared at me as if I were Tarzan in the middle of New York City.  The rabbi said, "Continue singing, children!"  When they finished, he approached me.  He was a very old man and reminded me of a rabbi I had known when I was a child in Poland.  He asked, "Where are you from?" and I told him that I had come in from the street because I heard the class singing.  I asked, "Why are you singing a song of such deep grief and exile?"  He replied, "Simply because I like it."

I then told him, "When I was the age of these children—in 1938, before the Holocaust—I sang that song many times.  But I don't sing it anymore because I have believed in God, and now I know that the Lord will never hide His face from me.  Of course, we all have hidden our faces from God, and then, when He does not answer our prayers, we think it is His fault.  But no!  The fault is ours.  God is merciful, and people can come close to Him by following what is written in Psalm 50:15, 'call upon me in the day of trouble; I will deliver thee, and thou shalt glorify me.'  Since the time I believed in the Lord, I no longer have to ask Him, 'Why do you hide your face from me and forget me?' "  I continued to read from the Psalms, praising God with joy in my heart.  I explained that I am free to ask the Lord to forgive my iniquities and that He is always ready to do so.

As I spoke with the rabbi, the children sat quietly, listening to our conversation.  Watching them brought another Scripture passage to my mind, and I read it to them: "Unto thee, O LORD, do I lift up my soul…Remember not the sins of my youth" (Ps. 25:1, 7).

At this point the rabbi asked the children, "What do you think? Should we continue our lesson or listen to what this man has to say?" There were about 40 children in the class, all boys with long side curls. A few years ago I had an opportunity to speak in an Orthodox school for girls, but in this school for boys I felt as if I were in the lions' den. I silently prayed in my heart, "O Lord, guide me, give me the words to say." At the same time, the rabbi called several other rabbis—all teachers—into the lecture hall.

I then began to speak to them, first telling them about myself— my life in Poland before the war, my experiences during the Holocaust, how I lost my entire family in the Warsaw Ghetto and the concentration camps, my time in the internment camps on Cyprus, my arrival in Israel, and my participation in all the wars through 1973. I went slowly, step by step, right up to the present time. Then I began to tell them about my faith. I could not start by declaring that I believe in Jesus Christ. I wanted them to mention His name first. I quoted several passages from Isaiah, Micah, and other prophets about the Messiah, all the while waiting for the outcry, the outburst of temper, the threats when they realized I was speaking about Jesus. I did not have to wait long. One of the teachers soon asked, "What books have you read?" I responded, "Do you see what I have in my hand? It is the Holy Bible, the book I love best and the only one I use. Is it a sin to love God's Word?"

I continued to speak for about 35 minutes, and everyone—students and teachers alike—listened carefully. When I finished, they began to ask questions. "Why did you come here?" one of the students wanted to know. "Because of the sad song you were singing," I replied. "I felt sorry for you, and I wanted you to be able to rejoice in the Lord with me. The Jewish people have lamented long enough. The time has come to turn to the Lord, the one true God, and ask for His help.  As I told you before, it is written in Psalm 50:15, 'call upon me in the day of trouble; I will deliver thee, and thou shalt glorify me.'  If you call upon Him, you can say with Isaiah, 'we will be glad and rejoice in his salvation' [Isa. 25:9]." When the rabbis heard this, they looked at each other in silence.  It was as if someone had tied them up and put glue on their lips.

Shortly thereafter, I left the school with a very good feeling.  I believe that many of the ones I spoke to—students and teachers— were seriously considering the things I told them about the Lord.  I trust that they will read the Bible passages for themselves and see that the Lord alone can bring them out of sorrow and into joy and peace, if only they will trust Him as their Messiah and Savior.

—1994

## FROM SILENCE AND SORROW
## TO JOYFUL SINGING

My wife and I recently visited her mother in the hospital. Now past 90 years old, she is like most of the other people in that particular hospital. They can no longer care for themselves, spend most of their waking hours in wheelchairs, speak very little, and appear to be very bitter. There are no smiles on their lips and no indications that they enjoy life. Most of them seem to be counting the days until they die. As I viewed this sorrowful picture, I asked myself, Can it be that I was sent here, not only to visit my mother-in-law, but to bring encouragement to these other people as well?

I quickly befriended many of them, and several conversations ensued. These Jewish people had come from both Arab and European countries, and so I spoke with some in Arabic, with others in Yiddish, and with still others in European languages. They immediately seemed to like me, probably because I made them feel that they still have value in this life and that they are very important in the eyes of God. Soon there were expressions of happiness on their faces.

I asked them if they remembered anything about the Bible. Most replied that they pray only from their prayer books, and they said they sometimes have to listen, against their will, to rabbis who visit the hospital and tell the old stories and traditions handed down through the centuries. One of the men said, "Listening to the rabbis does not make us happy or bring us joy, but you, in just a short time, have actually made us smile."

I then read some verses from the Bible to show them that even in old age they can be fruitful. "I have been young, and now am old; yet have I not seen the righteous forsaken, nor his seed begging bread" (Ps. 37:25). "Thou shalt rise up before the hoary head, and honor the face of the old man, and fear thy God: I am the LORD" (Lev. 19:32). I went on to tell them, "You can see how important you are, even at your advanced age. And you can be even more important if you will turn back to the Lord. Don't dwell on your old age and your good deeds here on earth. Rather, return to the Lord and obey His commandments during whatever time you have left."

Now they began to pay close attention to what I was saying, but one elderly man asked, "Do you expect me to forget in one minute everything I have done in 96 years of life?" "Yes," I replied, "and it can be done if you will open your heart before the Almighty God and say, 'O God, forgive me.' As it is written in Jeremiah 31:34, 'saith the LORD…I will forgive their iniquity, and I will remember their sin no more.' " Many of them wanted to see for themselves where this verse was written, even though most have very poor eyesight, so I was glad to pass around the small Hebrew Bible I always carry with me.

In speaking with these people, I realized that most have been forsaken by their families, and, as I said before, they are unhappy and counting the hours until they leave this life. Unfortunately, none of them knows what the future holds. And so I continued to speak with them, telling them that they do not have to be bitter because anyone who truly believes in the Lord will never be forsaken by Him but will have everlasting life in His presence. As it is written in Job 19:25-26, "I know that my redeemer liveth, and that he shall stand at the latter day upon the earth; And though after my skin worms destroy this body, yet in my flesh shall I see God." I told them, "You must do as it is written in Amos 5:4, 'Seek ye me, and ye shall live.' In the Lord, there is no death—only life!"

As I read the Bible, I could tell from the expressions on their faces that they had never heard these things before. No one had ever given them any hope of joy in the Lord. They had been told things that brought only sorrow, which is why they were sitting in that place, looking so forlorn, counting the days and hours until the end. But when I started to speak with them, bringing them the message of joy in the Lord, they forgot about counting. Instead, they began to ask me questions about the future. They wanted assurance that the things I had told them were really true.

I then asked, "Do you believe what is written in the Psalms?" Many of them, especially the men, had spent many hours reading the Psalms, but they admitted, "We never paid much attention to what we read." I then started reading some of the Psalms to them— slowly, clearly, and loudly, so that their nearly deaf ears could hear. I ended with Psalm 23, putting special emphasis on the end of verse 6, "I will dwell in the house of the LORD forever." When I finished reading, some of them said, "We have read those passages many times, but they never entered into our hearts as they have today."

Just then, my wife said, "Zvi, today is Friday, and we must get to the shops before they close for the Sabbath." I looked at my watch and realized that I had been speaking with these people for more than three hours, but it seemed like such a short time. These elderly people seemed sad that I had to leave, and so I said to my wife, "Give me a few more minutes with my new friends." I then asked them, "Do you have any more questions before I leave?" One of them asked,

"How can you be so sure that you will 'dwell in the house of the LORD forever'?" I replied, "Everything I read was from the Holy Bible, which was written by the Holy Spirit of God. And, as it is written in Psalm 119:89, 'Forever, O LORD, thy word is settled in heaven.' If you do not believe in the living God, all you have to do is open your hearts to Him, put your trust in Him, and you will have the same assurance of the future. As it is clearly written in Psalm 118:17, 'I shall not die, but live, and declare the works of the LORD.' "

These people then started to sing a song of joy to the Lord. I was so thrilled that in a few short hours they had gone from silence and sorrow to joyful singing. I plan to return to the hospital and continue witnessing to these dear people. I pray that they will recognize the truth about the Lord and accept Him as their Messiah and Savior before their earthly journey is over. It would make me so happy to know that my new friends "will dwell in the house of the LORD forever."

—1994

# WORLDS APART

I recently was in Eilat, in the south of Israel, visiting my daughter and her family. Because it is located on the Dead Sea, Eilat is a popular resort area, and many people from Europe go there for the therapeutic value of the water.

Whenever I visit Eilat, I enjoy walking along the beach and meeting new people. Among the many I met on my recent visit were two men who did not seem particularly happy when I tried to strike up a conversation with them. They look disheveled, and when I tried to speak with them about faith in God, they became upset. "You can see the sorry state of our lives," one of them said. "How, then, can you speak to us about faith? You are nicely dressed and do not appear to have any troubles. We are worlds apart from someone like you. We have done so many bad things in our lives that God could never forgive us or forget our sins."

At that time, I took out my small Bible and read one of its most familiar verses: "For God so loved the world, that he gave his only begotten Son, that whosoever believeth in him should not perish, but have everlasting life" (Jn. 3:16). I then explained, "This passage does not say that God will accept people based on who they are or what they have done in the past. God said, 'whosoever,' and the only condition is that you believe on His Son. If you will accept the Lord Jesus as your Savior, God will immediately forgive and forget whatever you have done up to that point in your life, and He will give you the means of receiving forgiveness of any sins you commit in the future."

The man spoke up again, this time more earnestly. "We are very insignificant to God, and it will not help us now to come before Him and ask Him to forgive us." I then asked, "What in the world have you done? Did you kill someone?" "No," the other man said, "but we are poor and homeless. We live here on this beach, and we are so dirty that people hate to even look at us." I then read to them the comforting words of Psalm 118:22: "The stone which the builders refused is become the head of the corner." "Don't say that you are beyond hope, my friends," I told them. "Believe me, in God's sight you are of as much value as any other person ever born into this world. God's Son was rejected by the Jewish leaders, but God the Father did not reject Him. Rather, through His death and resurrection He became the Messiah and Savior of the world."

After more conversation they asked, "What do you want us to do?" I answered, "For me, you do not have to do anything. What you must do is for yourselves. You must come to God, worship Him, be faithful to Him, and bear fruit for His glory. If you do, I am sure you will no longer question who you are or say that you have no value before God. Instead, you will be glad to be called servants of the Lord. Regardless of what you see when you look in the mirror, you will be children of God and will never again doubt your worth before Him."

At that time they became more open with me, and, without my asking, they began to tell me about themselves. They were alcoholics and had lost their families, their homes, everything they ever had because of that evil bottle of vodka. They said, "There is no doctor who can cure us of this chronic disease." I responded "Quite to the contrary, it would be very easy for you to stop drinking." They were surprised and asked, "How?" "You do not have to go to a doctor. You can stop on your own," I replied. Becoming impatient, they again asked, "How? Tell us now!" I said, "Open your hearts before God. He will listen and answer your prayer. He will make it possible for you to turn from that poison—alcohol."

By now they were very curious about me and asked, "Are you a pastor, or something like that?" I replied, "No, I am not a pastor, but, as a believer in Christ, it is my obligation to go to people who are in trouble and try to help them. All I want to do is help you wean yourselves from your destructive addiction to alcohol." Again they asked, "What do we have to do?" I told them, "Open your hearts to God, and He will do the rest." "Shall we do it right here, or wait until we go to bed?" they asked. I could not tell if they were being serious or mocking, so I said, "You must understand that this decision is yours alone to make. God is full of love and compassion, and He is ready to forgive you. If you think you would be doing me a personal favor by asking God for forgiveness, you are making a big mistake. If you are not serious about this, I'll be glad to leave you alone." "No, we are very serious," they assured me.

"Good," I responded. "In that case, you can go to a quiet spot on this very beach and pray silently in your hearts, so that only God Himself can hear. You need not pray in a loud voice because, as it is written, 'man looketh on the outward appearance, but the LORD looketh on the heart' [1 Sam. 16:7]. And please understand that it is not because of me that you should pray to God, but because of your own needs. I will not listen to you. Just talk freely from your hearts to the Lord. Tell Him of your sins and ask Him to forgive you and become your Savior." "Will you wait here for us?" they asked, and I assured them I would.

The two men then walked along the beach until they found a spot with no people nearby.  I waited and watched for more than a half hour as they both sat quietly under the hot sun with their heads slightly bowed and very serious expressions on their faces.  Of course, as I waited I prayed that the Lord would open their eyes and hearts and draw them to Himself.

Eventually they got up and returned to me, and, praise God, that which I would not have believed when I first met them had truly happened.  They had come to the Lord of their own free will.  Whereas before they were without any hope in this life, they were now full of hope because they had put their trust in God.  These two men, who just a short time before appeared to have lost the image of God in which they were created, and looked no better than the dust of the earth, now wore happy expressions on their faces.  They were full of joy because the Lord had taken away their stony hearts and given them hearts of flesh (Ezek. 36:26).  The Lord had given them a new heart and a new Spirit—the Spirit of the living God—and they were rejoicing in Him.  And so, of course, was I!

—1994

# THE EXPERT

I often go to the Wailing Wall in Jerusalem.  Invariably I meet people who think that just by going there they will be saved because the *Halacha* (body of Jewish law supplementing the Scriptures and forming especially the legal part of the Talmud) says that the divine presence can always be found there.  Many people go to the Wall to read the Book of Psalms.  They arrive very early in the morning and read so fast that no one can understand them, so that they can return to their homes as soon as possible.

I recently saw a group of young men at the Wall who were engrossed in reading the Psalms in this manner, and I noticed that one young man's Bible was opened to Psalm 24.  I interrupted him and asked if he understood what he was reading at supersonic speed. He replied, "It is my job to come here every day and read the Psalms, and for this I receive a monthly salary.  I am an expert at this.  Are you now trying to teach me how to read the Psalms? Believe me, I can do this with my eyes closed.  I don't even have to open the Bible."

I told him, "The Lord is not concerned with who can read the Psalms the fastest, or who can read them blindfolded. No, He is concerned with what is in your heart. The Lord would rather have you read only a few words, but with sincerity and from your heart, than read the entire book and not understand one word of it. I see that your Bible is open to a wonderful chapter—Psalm 24. Do you know the one about whom King David is speaking?"

At that point, the other young men around him entered the conversation, and they spoke among themselves, saying, "Let's take a good look at this passage." But after a few minutes they said to me, "Why should we break our heads trying to interpret this Psalm? Ask our rabbi. He will tell you everything you want to know." They then called to the rabbi, who came over to the group and immediately asked me, "What do you want with these young men? You should not bother them. They must continue to read the Psalms." I responded, "Rabbi, as a believer in God, I am against this distortion of facts and degrading of our God. You call on Him every day when you say the *Shmah Israel* ['Hear, O Israel: The LORD our God is one LORD,' Dt. 6:4], and yet here you read about Him as if you are not interested or do not even know who He is.

"In the Psalm where this young man's Bible is opened, it is written, 'Lift up your heads, O ye gates...and the King of glory shall come in. Who is this King of glory?' [Ps. 24:7-8]. Tell me, rabbi, do you know who this King of glory is? The passage goes on to say, 'The LORD strong and mighty, the LORD mighty in battle...The LORD of hosts, he is the King of glory' [Ps. 24:8, 10]. If you would read this Psalm— not at breakneck speed, but slowly, to understand the meaning—you would know the one about whom it is written, and you would believe in Him in the way in which He wants you to believe. Rabbi, all the time that you and these young men spend here at the Wailing Wall is nothing more than what King Solomon said in Ecclesiastes 1:2: 'Vanity of vanities, saith the Preacher, vanity of vanities; all is vanity.' "

Now all of the young men began to look at the rabbi, wondering how he would respond. To them, the conversation had become a competition between the two of us to see who knew more about the Scriptures. But that was not my intention. In every situation, I put my trust in the Lord, confident that through His Holy Spirit He will put the right words in my mouth.

The rabbi thought for a long time and finally asked, "Who gave you the authority to come here and tell these people how to read the Psalms?" I replied, "The authority I have is available to you and everyone else in this world, but in order to have it you must receive the Lord as your Savior. You think that you have a relationship with God, but you are only playing games. You are probably not familiar with Ezekiel 33, but if you read that chapter you will learn who gave me the authority and responsibility to come here and warn wicked people, like yourselves, to turn to the Lord."

The rabbi was no longer quiet. He shouted, "How can you say that I am wicked?" "Because you worship idols and dance around the golden calf," I replied. "But I worship the living God. I never sacrifice a chicken as a personal offering for my sins on Yom Kippur because it is written in Isaiah 53 that the Lord is my atonement."

As soon as I mentioned Isaiah 53, the *forbidden* chapter, there were no more secrets between us. They immediately realized that I believe in Christ and am, in their opinion, an *apostate*. They did not understand, however, how I could believe in Him and yet put my trust in the Bible as the foundation of my faith. Such a thought was making them crazy, and I knew that the time had come for me to tell them about Him, to be a light to these men who were walking in darkness. The first thing I did—something I do all the time with such people—was ask them to look at my Bible to see if it is the true Hebrew Scriptures. The rabbi took it, examined it from front to back, and admitted, "Yes, this is our Bible." "Now that you know that," I said, "let me show you how I came to believe in

Christ—not according to any other book or books, such as the ones you study, but according to the facts given right here in God's living Word. This book was written by the Holy Spirit of God, and in it I found my Savior, the Lord Jesus Christ, the one whom you call 'this man.' "

I then began to read and expound the Scriptures to these Jewish men at the Wailing Wall, and our conversation lasted for several hours. I am sure that the seeds planted that day penetrated deep into the fertile ground of their souls, and I pray that those seeds will grow into understanding in their minds and hearts, so that they will one day come to know the Lord as their Savior.

—1995

# HOW DO YOU PRAY?

In these times of great uncertainty in Israel, the leaders of the *Cabala* (Jewish mysticism) rabbis have taken it upon themselves to compose a new prayer—a nice poem that will comfort the people. One of those rabbis is the leader of a large synagogue in my neighborhood. When we first met, he was not very friendly with me because he knows that I believe in Jesus as my Savior. For a long time he would not even look at me if we passed on the street, but when he learned from members of his synagogue that I often make repairs to their homes free of charge, he gradually changed his attitude toward me. We have since become good friends, but I always wonder how long that friendship will last.

When I met him recently, He was the first one to say "Shalom," and I knew immediately that he wanted my help. I was happy to do the work he requested, and, as always, I did not charge him for my services. When I was finished, he surprised me by asking, "Zvi, have you lost your head, believing in *this man* Jesus? And how did you come to your decision to believe in Him?" Because we were in his synagogue, I pointed to the extensive library and said, "Look at the many books you have here, but can you show me even one copy of the Bible, the Holy Scriptures? How can you call this a house of prayer when you do not have even one Bible here?"

He then told me, "You can see for yourself that most of the books here are prayer books. Even now, I and other rabbis are wracking our brains trying to compose a new prayer, a nice poem to comfort the people of Israel in these difficult days. In fact, I would be interested in any help you can offer in composing the new prayer." I replied, "I am not a writer, but I can give you some important help for this project. If you want to know how to really pray to God, you must ask Him directly for His help. All of the composed poems and prayers in the world will not help you. They are nothing more that what King Solomon said in Ecclesiastes 1:2, 'Vanity of vanities…all is vanity.' So also are all of your prayer books and this effort to write a new poem or prayer. It will be of no more help than cupping a glass for the dead or giving eyeglasses to a blind horse. If the prayer does not come from the depths of your heart, it is, as I just said, nothing more than vanity. Even you, a rabbi in a large synagogue, cannot turn people into robots. Each person is free to come before God and open his or her heart to Him. You must not tell them how to pray. Remember, you can kill the body, but never the spirit."

The rabbi was listening intently, as never before, and then he asked, "How do you pray? With what words do you start?" I then opened my Bible to Psalm 25 and read, "Unto thee, O LORD, do I lift up my soul. O my God, I trust in thee…Show me thy ways, O LORD; teach me thy paths…for thou art the God of my salvation" (vv. 1-2, 4-5). I then told him, "These are the words of King David. He prayed to God and said all that was in his heart, without worrying about whether it was a nice poem. He knew all the sins he had committed against God's will, and so, in another prayer, he said, 'Cast me not away from thy presence, and take not thy holy Spirit from me' [Ps. 51:11]. You can see that the Holy Spirit of God was very important to David. Also, he humbled himself before God, yet you want to come before Him with great words and fancy poems. Listen to what King David said to God when he prayed: 'Have mercy upon me, O LORD; for I am weak' [Ps. 6:2]; and again, 'Teach me thy way, O LORD, and lead me in a plain path, because of mine enemies' [Ps. 27:11].

"David uttered all of these words, not because he was a great poet, but because he was a great sinner. I am not suggesting that you copy his words as your new prayer, but you can use David's words as an example of his simplicity and humility before God."

The rabbi then asked, "How do believers in Jesus pray?" I replied, "As I said before, we never pray from books that have been written by others. We only pray what is on our hearts at any given time, in any given situation. This ability comes through the Holy Spirit of God as people place their faith and trust in the Lord Jesus. Believe me, you do not have to be a great poet or compete with others to see who can write the nicest words. Your prayers must come from the depths of your heart, and the words you use do not matter to God. In fact, you do not even have to speak out loud. Hannah prayed silently in the Temple at Shiloh, but her petition came from deep within her heart. God heard her prayer and gave her the desire of her heart, and the result was the birth of Samuel.

"Believers in Jesus do not have prayer books or pray special prayers on special occasions. We come before God Almighty with open hearts, and He answers our prayers according to His holy will. This is what God wants from His children. He has said in Ezekiel 36:26, 'A new heart also will I give you, and a new spirit will I put within you; and I will take away the stony heart out of your flesh, and I will give you an heart of flesh.' "

The rabbi was surprised that I read from the Bible because he was sure that believers in Jesus did not use the Bible. Finally, his eyes have begun to open to the truth about those of us who have trusted Jesus as our Messiah and Savior. He told me, "I have learned much today, but the distance between us is still very great." I said, "You must not try to bridge the distance between you and me, but between yourself and God. As it is written in Isaiah 53, He was bruised for our sins and crushed for our iniquities, and because of all that He has done for us, we must come to Him in the way He has directed in His Word."

The rabbi and I parted on a very friendly basis that day. I trust I will have many more opportunities to speak with him about the Lord Jesus, and in the meantime I have put the matter in God's hands, trusting Him to do a work in this man's heart.

—1995

## THE DESPAIR CORPS

Often I go out among people in public places. You can usu-ally tell a little something about them by looking at their faces, but only the people themselves know what is in their minds and hearts.

I recently visited a synagogue where many men, all with long beards and long curls, were studying the Talmud and other books of commentary. By Israeli standards, they looked religious—but were they really? Most of these men were young, and many were fairly open and engaged me in a long conversation about faith in God. They were very friendly to me, until I asked them, "Why do you come here day after day and spend your time with nothing but vanity?" Then they became suspicious, and one of them said, "I was a high-ranking officer in the army, but now I am happy to say that I have been here studying for three long years." I asked, "After those three long years of study, what do you know? Do you feel good about what you are doing?" He replied, "I come here to puri-fy my soul." I then said, "Take a good look at yourself in the mirror, and then tell me how you feel. Tell me if you truly think you have purified your soul."

He looked at me rather strangely and asked. "Have you ever served in the army?" "Yes," I replied. He went on, "I was a fighter pilot, and it was hard, but now I am like a bird with no wings. And do you know why? It is because I have come here to repent. Most of the others here have the same background. They were officers and good fighters, but now they are weak before God."

"You are all making a great mistake," I told him. "Why?" he asked. "Because you are like helpless sheep who have gone astray, following false teachers," I replied. "You are always looking to see who has the longest beard, because he is more righteous than the others. And the one with the longest curls—he too is more righteous. But you are all full of bitterness. You have no joy, no life, and, of course, no hope. If you continue to seek such 'purity' for yourselves, believe me, you will end up drowning in this cesspool of false teaching. Then it will be too late. Your pious outward appearance is like a costume children wear on Purim. Open your eyes and see how far you have fallen. You are so lost that you will never be purified if you stay here. Your only hope is to turn to God in the way He desires. Think about it."

As I spoke with this pilot and some of the others, they seemed to be listening intently. Then the chief rabbi of the synagogue came into the room, and he too listened carefully—for a while. I could tell just by looking at him that he was also a member of this *despair corps*. Finally he spoke up and said, "I am the chief rabbi of this place. You can see the great success we have had. You too may feel free to come here often. Our door is always open." I replied, "I know where my place is, and it is not here among those who are committing spiritual suicide. It is plain to see that there is no life here. Can you show me even one person who is happy, who is looking forward to the future? No, you can't! This place is like an open grave. The people are spending their lives in emptiness and vanity."

The rabbi heard me out, and then he responded, "I have been listening to you for quite a while now, and I want to know from which books you have taken the stories you are telling these men." I replied, "Everything I have said is from the Bible. It is written in Ezekiel 36:25-27, 'Then will I sprinkle clean water upon you, and ye shall be clean; from all your filthiness, and from all your idols, will I cleanse you. A new heart also will I give you, and a new spirit will I put within you; and I will take away the stony heart out of your flesh, and I will give you an heart of flesh. And I will put my Spirit within you, and cause you to walk in my statutes, and ye shall keep mine ordinances, and do them.' "

The rabbi took the Bible from me and examined it. It was then he realized that my Bible contained both the Old and New Testaments. He said, "This is not a surprise to me. As soon as I heard you speak, I knew that you were one of those who believe in *that man* [Jesus]—you are one of those people whom I do not like. But because you had the great courage to come here and tell us all that you believe, I must admit that I respect you. Now I challenge you to show me, from our Hebrew Scriptures only, where I have gone astray. Can you do that?"

I told him, "You are not alone in thinking that *that man*, as you call Him, is written about only in the New Testament, which you call a Christian book. That is why God has made the truth about Him so plain for us in Isaiah 53, a passage that is well-known among Jews around the world, and you cannot deny it. You say that you are waiting for salvation to come through the Messiah, but you are looking to the wrong people, such as the rabbi from New York [Menachem Schneerson], whom you all thought was the Messiah. Where is he now? In a grave in New York!"

I was sure that after saying these things, I would not be able to stand on my feet, thinking that these men would become physical with me.  Instead, I was surprised to find that after a long discussion, they were still very friendly to me.  Even the rabbi said, "Because you have been so open and seem so sure of your beliefs, I would be happy to have you come back for a longer discussion. You are welcome anytime."  This was a real fulfillment of the Lord's words in Luke 10:3, "behold, I send you forth as lambs among wolves."  These people need our prayers, and so do I as I plan to visit them again very soon.

—1995

## HOW CAN YOU BE SAVED?

In Isaiah 1:2 it is written, "I have nourished and brought up children, and they have rebelled against me."

I was recently waiting at the bus stop to go into town, and a very old gentleman was standing in line with me. When the bus came along, I noticed that he needed help to board, so I assisted him and sat next to him on the short ride into Jerusalem. During the ride, I asked how old he was, and he replied, "I am much too old—94!" I then asked, "Why are you going into town by yourself?" He said, "As it is written in the Talmud, in Aboth 1:14, 'If I am not for myself, who is for me?' " "Where are your children?" I asked, and he answered, "If I waited for my children to help me get into town, I would never get there."

I then asked, "Do your children go to the synagogue?" "Of course," he replied. "They are all like me—law-observing, sin-fearing people." "If that is so," I said, "then how do they feel about what is written in Exodus 20:12, 'Honor thy father and thy mother, that thy days may be long upon the land which the LORD thy

God giveth thee'?  Are they doing this?  Are they honoring you?"
He replied, "It is very hard these days to find such children."  I told
him, "If, as you say, your children observe the law, where are they
now when you need them?"

At about that time, we arrived at our destination, and as I helped
him from the bus, I said, "If your children were really following the
commands of the Lord, they would not leave you alone."  He said,
"I cannot do anything for myself.  I am 94 years old, and everyday
I wait for the end.  I have no hope!"  I then told him what King
David said in his time of trouble:  "Cast me not away from thy presence, and take not thy holy Spirit from me" (Ps. 51:11).  I went on
to say, "Even in your old age, you can be fruitful for the Lord, as it
is written in Psalm 92:14, 'They shall still bring forth fruit in old
age; they shall be fat and flourishing.' "

This elderly man commented, "I know the entire Book of
Psalms by rote, but I never thought about that portion before."  I
responded, "That is because you know the book *by heart*, but you
do not have it *in your heart*.  Therefore, you don't remember the
most important words of the Lord, and you do not know what He
expects of us."

We spoke for a long time, then he asked, "Do you go to the synagogue often?"  "No," I replied.  "If that is so, then how do you
pray?" he asked.  I answered, "From the depths of my heart, and the
Lord hears and answers my prayers.  I do not read prayers that have
been written for me by other people."

I then told him, "I have four adult children, and every one of
them respects my wife and me as their mother and father.  This is
because they worship the living God rather than following false
teachers."  He then asked, "What do you call your synagogue?"  I
replied, "As it is written in Isaiah 56:7, we call it a 'house of prayer.'
We know that if our prayers come from deep within our hearts,
rather than out of books, the Lord will hear and answer us."

Then he really opened his heart and said, "I have five children, and not one of them brings me any satisfaction as a father." I said, "Our God is a God of love and mercy, and He will bestow His love and mercy on those who will receive Him." I then read John 3:16: "For God so loved the world, that he gave his only begotten Son, that whosoever believeth in him should not perish, but have everlasting life." He listened very carefully and then asked where this passage was written. I told him it was from the New Testament and immediately read to him about the love and mercy of God from Isaiah 53:5 and 10: "But he was wounded for our transgressions, he was bruised for our iniquities; the chastisement for our peace was upon him, and with his stripes we are healed…Yet it pleased the LORD to bruise him; he hath put him to grief."

Suddenly it seemed as if this old man were young again. He was so interested in what God had done for us and asked why He would do this. He asked many questions and listened carefully to my answers from the Scripture. I took him, step by step, through the plan of salvation, using mostly Old Testament Scriptures because he was not familiar with the New Testament. We were sitting in a public park, and although he was much older than I, he listened—hanging onto my every word—like a youngster in school.

Finally he asked, "How can it be that I have read these passages so many times over the years, and none of this meaning ever came into my mind?" I opened the Bible for him, and although he is 94 years old, with the help of glasses he can see very clearly and read some of the passages for himself. Then he said, "I wonder why, over these many years, I have never studied Isaiah 53." I told him, "It is because your false leaders have discouraged you from doing so. They don't even read it in the synagogues."

This elderly man had a long white beard and looked like he could have been one of the ancient prophets of Israel. But inside he was empty. Everyone calls him "Rabbi" to honor him, and I also spoke to him with respect because of his great age. Perhaps that was why he started to ask questions about subjects he had never considered before. I told him, "You cannot be saved by killing a chicken, which the religious Jews do on the Day of Atonement. As it is written in Isaiah 52:3, 'For thus saith the LORD, Ye have sold yourselves for nothing, and ye shall be redeemed without money.' "

Because of the importance of this verse, I let him read it for himself. Finally he asked, "Then how can you be saved?" I replied, "Through the blood of our Savior, Jesus Christ." Again I read to him the entire 53rd chapter of Isaiah, so that it would root itself deeply into his mind and, even more importantly, into his heart.

After spending several hours together in the public park, I led him back to the bus stop. When we parted, he said, "I will never forget our time together. Thank you!" I pray that as he reads the Scriptures now, the Spirit of God will open his eyes and heart and that he will come to salvation while there is still time.

—1996

## LIFE AFTER DEATH

A few years ago, I read an account in the newspaper of a lady who was celebrating her one hundredth birthday. From her picture and the interview, she seemed to be a nice person. When asked if she was afraid to die and if she believed in life after death, she replied, "I am very jealous of those Christians, who believe in life after death, and they are so sure of themselves. I am not that sure."

Shortly after I read that story, I learned that a well-known rabbi was going to speak in one of Jerusalem's big synagogues. His topic? Life after death. Naturally, I was curious about his thoughts on the subject, and I decided to attend the meeting.

During the question and answer session following his message, the rabbi and I engaged in a rather heated discussion because I told him, in front of several hundred people, that a person can have eternal life only through faith in the Lord Jesus Christ. Finally he said to me, "I never want to see you at one of my meetings again!" But I never give up quickly, and I replied, "When you come to speak here again, you will see my shadow."

Recently I saw posters on the streets announcing that this rabbi was going to speak in the area, and I kept my word. What's more, I sat on the front bench. When he took the platform, he began to speak about many great rabbis who had gone before him. He said that they are all in heaven now, enjoying the benefits of eternal life. He spoke for more than an hour before he realized that I was there, but as soon as he spotted me, he became tongue-tied and confused. The people in the audience were surprised at his change in demeanor. He then ended his speech abruptly, without bringing his remarks to a proper conclusion.

Many people requested a question and answer session, and the rabbi said, "I am in a hurry, but I will answer one or two brief questions." I was the first one to stand up, and I asked him, "How can you be so sure you will have life after death when you have ignored the commands of God? You, as a rabbi, should know better." The people were surprised to hear such a question asked of a rabbi, and they were very interested to hear how he would reply. The rabbi looked intently at me and asked, "Do you remember what I told you a few years ago? I told you that you and I were in the past, and we are now living in the present."

Some of the people in the audience asked, "What is going on here?" Of course, the rabbi wanted the audience to support him, so he began to accuse me of idolatry. When he was finished, I held up my Bible for everyone to see and said, "Here is the Holy Bible, and I worship the Lord according to it. Is this, as the rabbi says, idolatry?" I then asked the rabbi to show the audience the book he was using. Naturally, it was one of the multitude of commentary books, and not the Bible. I then asked the people, "Which book is more kosher? And who is practicing idolatry?"

I thank the Lord that I was not afraid, even though I was standing in the lions' den. I always remember the words of Luke 12:11-12, "And when they bring you unto the synagogues, and unto magistrates, and powers, be not anxious how or what thing ye shall answer, or what ye shall say; For the Holy Spirit shall teach you in the same hour what ye ought to say." Because these words are always with me, I can face whatever comes my way.

The rabbi had some of his people with him, and they started to contend with me. But I have eaten that kind of food before, and I know how it tastes. I began to explain my position very slowly, and I could sense that the people were interested to know why I had come to the meeting. I told them, "I believe, according to the law, that we are the Chosen People of God. It is our duty to go to people and preach the gospel about the Lord. We are not to teach a false gospel, but the truth from the Bible. You can see that I have no other books with me—no commentary books written by great sages, who were, after all, just men. I am not afraid to open any portion of the Bible. I never cover certain pages so people cannot see what is written there. With what has this great rabbi come to you tonight? He has come with fictitious stories, and most of you accepted what he said, although you do not really understand what he means. But one day you will know, and then it may be too late. I encourage you all to go home and read the Bible. Do not skip over the parts that don't interest you or chapters that the rabbis have told you not to go near. Read it all; read all the commands of God. Then you will know how to worship Him, and you will know how to obtain true eternal life."

Then some of the people asked, "Who is your God?" I replied, "He is not *my* God. He is *our* God. He is one God for all the world, and He is the Savior, *Yeshua Hamashiah*." I said His name in Hebrew because if I had said it in English—Jesus Christ—that would not have been kosher enough for them. "You can read about Him in the Bible," I told them. "It is because of what I read about Him in the Hebrew Scriptures that I have believed in Him as my Savior, and you can do the same thing."

A few people asked to examine my Bible to see if it was the complete Hebrew Scriptures. I let them look at it as long as they wished, and then I asked, "What do you think? Have I come to you with fictitious stories, like this rabbi, or with the living facts about the Lord our God?"

By then the rabbi had had enough of this discussion, and he left. I, however, stayed and had some very good conversations about the Lord. I pray that what they heard that night—not from the rabbi but from the Word of God—will penetrate their minds and hearts and lead them to a true knowledge of the living Savior. It is all there for them to read, in black and white, if they will just do their part.

—1996

## AN HISTORIC MEETING

Many times I go to the Ultra-Orthodox yeshivas and engage the people in long discussions, trying to bring them back to their roots, back to the Bible. They, in turn, always show me the many books from their *Halacha*, or traditions—literature written over the centuries by the great rabbis of old. They gather round me like sharks and try to convince me that only through the Halacha can I be saved and be a "good Jew" like them. Of course, they are very serious in their beliefs, but some of them are curious and listen to what I have to say.

I always listen politely to their arguments from the Halacha, but when they finish, I tell them that they are all fictitious stories. I recently told one group of Ultra-Orthodox people, "These are nothing but stories such as I used to tell my children when they were young, and then they would go to sleep. Now you are trying to convince me that these stories are like 'good news.' I am sure that many people believe what you say, but not me!"

At that time an elderly man approached me. He had a long beard that was as white as snow, and people treated him with great respect, as if he were the Prophet Elijah. We looked at each other for a while, and finally he shouted out, "Zvi! Don't you know me?" I continued to look at him but did not recognize him. Then he said, "I know you very well. We spent a lot of time together—good times and hard times." I thought, Who can this man be? Then he said, "You must have lost your memory if you don't know me." I replied, "It is obvious that on the outside I have not changed much because you recognized me so quickly. But I have changed on the inside. As it is written in Ezekiel 36:26, 'A new heart also will I [the Lord] give you, and a new spirit will I put within you; and I will take away the stony heart out of your flesh, and I will give you an heart of flesh.' I can see that you have definitely changed on the outside, what with all this camouflage of clothing, long beard, and side curls, but you still have the same heart of stone because you are here in this place. I don't remember knowing anyone in the past who looked like you. How can you expect me to recognize you?"

Finally he identified himself. And who was this great *holy one*? He was a man with whom I had served in the army in 1948. In fact, we had the same job, diffusing mines in the minefields. Together we witnessed death many times, and we were indeed good friends. Now here we were, meeting again after 48 years. Many of his friends were very much against me at the beginning of our conversation, but after our *historic* meeting, they all wanted to know about our lives from 1948 to 1996.

This man is 15 years older than I, and he is now 80 years old. He said, "Zvi, I have heard about you on many occasions over the years, but I never believed the things my friends told me about you. Now I can see with my own eyes and hear with my own ears that all of those reports were true. How did you come to such a decision? How could you leave the faith of our fathers and go about preaching something that is against our great rabbis, against the Halacha, against our traditions? How did this ever happen?"

Now all of the other Hasidim in the area gathered around us. They were interested to hear what I would say, how I would answer him. Every word that came out of my mouth was very important to them.

First I said, "I do not wish to speak against anyone. Rather, I am here to remind you to whom you belong. As it is written in Malachi 3:7, 'Even from the days of your fathers ye are gone away from mine ordinances, and have not kept them. Return unto me, and I will return unto you, saith the LORD of hosts.' The great rabbis did not say that; it was inspired by the Lord and written by His prophet. In fact, your great rabbis are not even mentioned in the Bible. There you will read only about the Lord God and what He has done for us. I have not come to you with fictitious stories. You can see that the only book I have with me is the Bible. Don't you wonder why I could not recognize you, although we were once such good friends, and you recognized me so easily? What is the big difference between us? Everyone here knows that you have changed your face, changed your style of dress, but you have not changed your heart. You still have a heart of stone. I, on the other hand, have not changed my appearance from the way I looked when we knew each other—except, of course, that I am almost 50 years older. But God has given me a heart of flesh, and that is the great difference between us. I have not changed His laws or His commands, as you have done."

My old friend then asked, "How can you say things like that?" I replied, "I have not said it. You can see with your own eyes, right here in the Holy Bible, that God Himself has said it. But it appears that mine is the only Bible in this place. Here, in your house of prayer, you have hundreds of books—maybe even thousands—but you do not have one copy of the Bible. So, where is your God? In all those books? It is written in Psalm 42:3, 'My tears have been my food day and night, while they continually say unto me, Where is thy God?'

"I worship the Lord according to the way He has commanded, and I have come here to warn you about the false teachings you are following. I pray that I am not too late. This is my obligation before God and all people. You can see this in black and white in Ezekiel 3:17: 'Son of man, I have made thee a watchman unto the house of Israel; therefore, hear the word at my mouth, and give them warning from me.' "

When I read from the Bible, they looked at it very carefully to be sure that I was not lying to them because they were very suspicious of me. But by the end of our conversation they said, "Even though we know about you and your beliefs, you are very interesting, and we would welcome you back to speak with us again."

I was grateful to the Lord for the good conclusion to our meeting, and I pray that I will have more opportunities to tell these people—and my old friend—how to have true faith in the Lord God. I pray that it is not too late to reach them with the good news about their Messiah.

—1996

## OUT OF ZION
## SHALL GO FORTH THE LAW

Over the years, the Lord has taught my wife and me to have an open-door policy in our home. People are coming and going all of the time, and some even sleep here—for one night or many nights. Once each year an elderly gentleman from Germany visits Israel. He does not come to see us only—he has many friends here—but he usually ends up sleeping at our home.

When he visited this year he said, "Zvi, I am not getting any younger. I am 80 years old now, and before I die I want you and your wife to visit me in Germany, even if only for a few days. I want to repay some of the kindness you have shown me over the years." This was the first time my wife had been outside of Israel in 48 years, but, as it is written in Ecclesiastes 11:1, "Cast thy bread upon the waters; for thou shalt find it after many days." And so, off we went to Germany.

This man is a true believer in Christ, and when we arrived he had arranged a great surprise for me. I was invited to speak at an assembly where most of the people are Russian immigrants. There were approximately 400 people in attendance, and because I can speak both German and Russian, this meeting presented a wonderful opportunity to speak with them about faith in Christ. After I spoke, many of the people asked what it is like to be a believer in Israel. I replied, "As it is written in Mark 16:15, we are to 'Go…into all the world, and preach the gospel to every creature.' This is what I do, right there in Israel—and now here in Germany."

While many of the people present were believers and very receptive to what I was saying, I was reminded once again of King Solomon's words, "there is no new thing under the sun" (Eccl. 1:9). You see, there were a few Jews in the crowd who were just as stiff-necked as their brethren in Israel. As soon as they made their presence known, I knew what they were going to ask because I have heard the same things from such people time and time again over the years. "Did you come here to make us Christians?" they asked. "How can this be, especially from someone who is from Jerusalem?"

I replied, "I have come here to make you good Jews. I want you to turn back to the Bible, to your roots, and then you will know the whole truth about the Lord and what He expects of us as His children. He wants us to be His servants and to tell of His salvation to the ends of the earth. Because you do not know what the Bible is really about and, of course, you do not believe in the Lord Jesus Christ as your Savior, I am not surprised that you asked me such questions. Now that you have heard the truth, if you do not turn to the Lord, you are responsible for yourselves before God. I have done my duty, as it is written in Ezekiel 33:7-9: 'So thou, O son of man, I have set thee a watchman unto the house of Israel; therefore, thou shalt hear the word at my mouth, and warn them from me. When I say unto the wicked, O wicked man, thou shalt surely die; if thou dost not speak to warn the wicked from his way, that wicked man shall die in his iniquity, but his blood will I require at thine hand. Nevertheless, if thou warn the wicked of his way to turn from it, if he do not turn from his way, he shall die in his iniquity, but thou hast delivered thy soul.' "

These men spoke a little German, but most of our conversation was in Russian. This was the first time that a person from Israel had spoken to them about Christ and, what's more, in their own language.

My host had another surprise for me during our visit to Germany. One day two of the leaders from the assembly where I preached visited us, and I recognized them immediately. They had come to Israel a few years before and had stayed in our home. They are Russian immigrants to Germany. When they visited me in Israel, I knew that they were believers, but they never mentioned that they were leaders in an assembly with more than 400 members. They have lived near the town of Hanover for several years now, but they still do not know the German language. A long time ago, I wondered why it was that I was able to learn so many languages. Now I can see that being fluent in nine languages is not enough, considering the many people I have met and witnessed to over the years.

It was a great blessing for me, a Jew from Israel, to preach about our Savior Jesus Christ to so many people and to meet two of the leaders of this wonderful assembly. I encouraged them to continue reading the Bible and trusting in the Lord. I told them, "You would be surprised how many believe in Him as their Savior among our own people, the Jews. The apostles and the first believers were all Jews, and they believed what is written in Deuteronomy 18:15: 'The LORD thy God will raise up unto thee a Prophet from the midst of thee, of thy brethren…unto him ye shall hearken.' When we trust in the Lord and His Word, we always move ahead spiritually, never backward."

Just as the stiff-necked people in Jerusalem always want to see for themselves what I am speaking about from the Bible, so these Jews in Germany were no different. Again, this was not a surprise to me because I realized that most of them had probably never owned a

Bible.  When German believers spoke with them about Christ, they would not believe them because they were Gentiles and were using what they refer to as the "Gentile Bible."  Of course, I was glad to show them my Hebrew language Bible, so that they could see for themselves that I was not making up the words I was preaching to them.  It was all from the Word of God.

There is a saying in Yiddish, "How can a cat cross the sea?"  Likewise, how can a Jew from Jerusalem go to another country and preach the gospel of Christ.  It seems impossible, but it happened.  I am not saying that every day was like a carnival.  We were in Germany for two weeks, and there were some rough days, but the good times far outweighed the bad.  I was thrilled that the Lord gave me the special privilege of preaching to so many people, many of whom had never heard the good news of salvation in Jesus Christ.  Truly, as it is written in Isaiah 2:3, "out of Zion shall go forth the law, and the word of the LORD from Jerusalem."  And so we saw that our trip to Germany was not in vain.  The Lord brought forth much fruit, for which we sincerely thank Him.

Now I want to share with you some special news from our family.  My wife and I are again happy grandparents following the birth of twins girls to one of our sons and his dear wife.  The Lord has now blessed us with eleven grandchildren through our four children.  As it is written in Genesis 1:28, "Be fruitful, and multiply."  The Lord has answered our prayers in so many wonderful ways—through our family and through the opportunity to preach His salvation to the ends of the earth.  It is a great joy to listen to such a symphony from the Lord—a symphony that will never end.

—1996

# BUTCHER THE JEWS!
# CAST THEM INTO THE SEA!

It is obvious from observing the international scene that most of the world is against God's Chosen People, Israel. This nation occupies a very small piece of real estate—so small that it is hard to find on a map—yet it is the subject of more newspaper headlines and media reports worldwide than any other nation. The reason for this animosity is jealousy. As it is written in Song of Solomon 8:6, "love is strong as death, jealousy is cruel as sheol." In Deuteronomy 7:6 Moses said to the Israelites, "the LORD thy God hath chosen thee to be a special people unto himself, above all people who are upon the face of the earth." The problem is that the other nations want to be the special people. They do not want to admit that the Jewish nation was chosen by God above them. In many places in the Bible, the Jewish people are told not to fear. As the Lord God protected us from Pharaoh in Egypt long ago, so He will protect us from our present-day enemies.

Now we are in a situation such as the children of Israel faced when Pharaoh chased them to the Red Sea. We are surrounded by Arab nations whose favorite slogan is, "Butcher the Jews! Cast them into the sea!" But our motto cannot be the same. We must never repay them with the coin of hatred. We must show them that there are many ways in which we can be friendly with each other. Of course, the chief way—the only real way—is through the love of Christ. Everyone who believes in Him will see the kingdom of God. This cannot be accomplished with the sword on the field of slaughter, but with love.

Many times I have the opportunity to speak with my Arab neighbors. It is the same with them as it is with the Ultra-Orthodox Jews. We sometimes speak for many hours before we get around to the most important subject of all, faith in Christ. When I speak with Arabs, the first thing I must do is draw them away from their blind hatred—their long-standing, deadly hatred of the Jewish people. Then we can begin to speak about faith in Christ. Most of the Arabs I speak with are young people, and it is very hard to explain to them the meaning of the word *love* because they grew up on the words of Genesis 27:40, "by the sword shalt thou live." I must go very slowly with these people, but eventually, even without the sword, we can come to an understanding.

Because we live near one another, I see them often, and they are usually interested in continuing our dialogue about faith in Christ. Recently when we met, my neighbors had with them a sheikh, one who knows the Koran. I spoke with him, but, as we all know, not every prophet is of the same mind. He began by asking, "Where is it written in the Torah that this land belongs to the Jews?" He was so sure of himself, certain that the Torah did not state such a thing. Quickly I showed him Genesis 13:14-17, where the Lord promised the land of Israel to Abraham and his descendants forever. At that time, Abraham resided in Hebron, which was part of the land grant given to him and his descendants by the Lord. I then showed them other places in the Torah where the borders of Israel are given, such as Genesis 15:18 and Exodus 23:31.

As I spoke with them that day, I remembered 2 Timothy 2:24, which states, "the servant of the Lord must…be…patient," because I realize that they do not accept such statements easily. And I was right! The sheikh immediately said, "That cannot be. The Koran says it is not so." I then said, "Go to your teachers and ask them when the Bible [the Torah] was written and when the Koran was written. They will have to tell you, in all honesty, that the Bible was written first, and it is the authentic Word of God."

There was another thing this sheikh could not accept. "How can you," he asked, "a Jew, speak about Christ?" I replied, "I believe in Him, not because someone told me to and I follow in blind faith. Rather, I believe as I do because Christ is written about in the Bible, in the Jewish Scriptures. It is my obligation, as a good Jew, to believe what is written there."

Then they began to ask me more questions, just as the Ultra-Orthodox Jews do. "Are you a Christian? Are you one of those who carries a big cross down the Via Dolorosa on Good Friday?" I answered, "I belong to the living God, and not to idols. I believe in the one who was pierced for our transgressions, as it is written in Isaiah 53:5. I am sure you will not find this in the Koran, which was written by a man. The Bible was written by the Holy Spirit of God, who spoke through the prophets."

By this time, more of my Arab neighbors had joined the group, and they seemed interested in what I was saying. I told them, "It is only through the power of the Lord that we can come together and speak with each other in a friendly manner. Perhaps one day all Arabs and Israelis will be able to come together and speak as we are doing now. Perhaps one day we will come to a mutual understanding without drawing the sword. As it is written in Isaiah 11:6, one day 'The wolf also shall dwell with the lamb, and the leopard shall lie down with the kid; and the calf and the young lion and the fatling together, and a little child shall lead them.' We are seeing something like that here today. But this prophecy can only be fulfilled when we all have a common faith in Christ, the only one who can give people the ability to put aside their differences and hatred and love and serve one another through Him."

Just as we are to take His Word to the Jewish people, so we are to take it to all the people of the world. Jesus commanded His disciples—and us—"Go ye into all the world, and preach the gospel to every creature" (Mk. 16:15), and this includes the Arabs. I pray that we will soon see a great harvest among them, as well as among the Jewish people here in His Holy Land.

—1997

# A SMALL MIRACLE

I have some of my best conversations with people at the bus stop or on the bus. One recent day I was waiting for the bus to go into Jerusalem, when two young men approached me and asked if I lived in the neighborhood. I told them I did, and they asked for directions to a synagogue, which I gladly gave them, telling them that it was very close by. They replied, "We want to pray, but we have already been to that synagogue, and it is locked up tight." I asked, "If every synagogue were locked up tight, would you not pray?"

They looked strangely at me and asked, "How can you pray without a *minyan* [ten people required to conduct a Jewish worship service]? It is impossible." I responded, "That is a mistake. You see, God is not looking to see if you pray in a synagogue. He looks at your heart. If you pray to Him from the depths of your heart, you can be sure that your prayer will be heard in heaven."

Again they looked strangely at me and asked, "How can you pray without a *tallit* [a prayer shawl] and without *tefillin* [phylacteries]?" I replied, "Those things are not important. To God, they are nothing more than a disguise. What the Lord wants from us is our hearts. You must realize that without the heart, there is no life. When we give God our hearts, we give Him ourselves, our very lives."

As we were talking, more people arrived at the bus stop, and most of them wanted to join the conversation. Some of the men belonged to the synagogue that was locked, and, because they know me, they asked, "Why are you always against everything we do? You know that for many years we have followed the old traditions. Who are you to say that they are not true? Why are you trying to brainwash these young men, so that they will leave the God of our fathers?" I said, "My duty is to bring them *closer* to God, and not according to the old traditions, but according to Zechariah 1:3: 'Turn unto me, saith the LORD of hosts, and I will turn unto you.' Zechariah also refers to your old traditions: 'Be not as your fathers, unto whom the former prophets have cried, saying, Thus saith the LORD of hosts: Turn now from your evil ways, and from your evil doings; but they did not hear, nor hearken unto me, saith the LORD' [Zech. 1:4]."

It was like a small miracle to me to be able to give them living facts from the Bible, and not examples from their old fictitious stories, as they always do. It was also a small miracle that the bus was late, giving me more time to tell these people the truth about God and how to open their hearts before Him.

Eventually the two young men said that they wanted to repent, and they asked me to take them to see the rabbi. I told them, "If you really want to repent, you do not need a rabbi. You can go before the Lord yourselves, individually, and open your hearts before Him. Believe me, you will know that you are saved from your sins. Then you will not have to wear those funny clothes, which make you look like you have come from another planet. It is enough for God when you come before Him and say, 'Lord, save me!' You can say, just as King David did in Psalm 25:1-2, 'Unto thee, O LORD, do I lift up my soul. O my God, I trust in thee; let me not be ashamed.' "

Sensing their great need, I read the remainder of Psalm 25, along with some other passages, including Jeremiah 31:33: "But this shall be the covenant that I will make with the house of Israel: After those days, saith the LORD, I will put my law in their inward parts, and write it in their hearts, and will be their God, and they shall be my people."

As soon as I spoke the word *covenant*, some of the older men said to the young men, "You must fear him. He is speaking from the New Testament, the book *those Christians* believe!" I told them how blind they were as I showed them that I had read from the Prophet Jeremiah and not from the New Testament, as they thought. All of these men were surprised. This was the first time that most of them had seen with their own eyes that the Jewish prophets spoke about the new covenant, and it was hard for them to believe.

Because we had come to the subject of the New Testament, I showed them some Old Testament passages that clearly speak of the Lord Jesus. By then, they all knew who I was and in whom I believe—the mighty God, and no one else.

I pray that I will have more opportunities to meet with these people, especially the two young men, and tell them how they can truly repent by putting their faith and trust in the Messiah of Israel.

—1997

# HANUKKAH—OR CHRISTMAS?

It is now the time of year when we Christians celebrate the Lord's birth and gladly sing, "Joy to the world! The Lord is come." In Israel, the people are also celebrating a holiday. For them it is the feast of Hanukkah, the Festival of Lights. I recently visited an Ultra-Orthodox school, where the holidays are faithfully kept, and I had a long conversation with some of the students about the feasts of Christmas and Hanukkah.

One student said, "Hanukkah is a very holy feast." I responded, "If that is so, why is it not mentioned even once in the Jewish Scriptures, and yet Christmas is mentioned several times there? Hanukkah is a feast that lasts for only a few days, and then the light of the festival goes out for another year. The people sink back into the darkness and depression that so often pervade this nation. On the other hand, those of us who celebrate Christmas have an everlasting light—not just some traditional candles that last for eight days, but a light in our hearts that never goes out. We celebrate and rejoice in the coming of the Lord, in whom there is no more darkness, no more sorrow. That is the great difference between these two feasts."

The pupils listened carefully as I spoke, but when I finished one of them said, "That is a nice story. Now show us where it is written in the Bible concerning this one about whom you speak." I told them, "I will be glad to show you passages that speak of Him, and then you must show me where the Bible speaks of the feast of Hanukkah." They quickly agreed because they were curious about what I would say and also because they wanted to trap me. But, as it is written in Psalm 9:15, "in the net which they hid is their own foot taken." I then read Isaiah 7:14: "Therefore the Lord himself shall give you a sign; Behold, the virgin shall conceive, and bear a son, and shall call his name Immanuel." They were glad I had referred to this passage because it didn't mention Bethlehem, and they thought they had trapped me in my speech. But then I read, in a very strong voice, Micah 5:2: "But thou, Bethlehem Ephrathah, though thou be little among the thousands of Judah, yet out of thee shall he come forth unto me that is to be ruler in Israel, whose goings forth have been from of old, from everlasting."

This made them uncomfortable, and they tried to divert my attention by discussing every word of the passage. Finally I said, "I did not come here to compete with you, to see who knows more Scripture or who is smarter. I am showing you the living facts that you yourselves asked to see, and you have seen it in black and white. Now the time has come for you to show me a passage from the Bible about Hanukkah, the Festival of Lights." This put them in an unpleasant position because they knew there was no reference to Hanukkah in the Scriptures. Therefore, they again tried to attack me because they were so sure that here, in their surroundings, I was as one in a lion's den. But even there I was not alone. The Lord was with me, and I knew that He would not forsake me. I put my trust in Him, and even among such *lions* I felt His strength.

This made them crazy, and one of them said, "You act as if you own this synagogue." I responded, "If you call this a house of prayer, as we call our place of worship, then it does belong to me—and to you, and to everyone else in the world. It should be a place where all people can come to worship their heavenly Father. He is not just *your* God, or *my* God. He is *our* God."

Finally, some of these young men began to show a little friendliness and sympathy toward me, and this was a very special feeling for me. But that feeling did not last for long. Soon a teacher entered the room, and one of the students told him what was happening. The teacher became angry with the students and said, "When the cat's away, the mice will play." He then came up to me and asked, "Who are you? Are you a teacher?" I replied, "It is not enough to be a teacher. Although I am not one, if I were, I would want to be considered an honest teacher. I can see that you and your colleagues are not being honest with your students.

"Many of these young people have spent the greater part of their lives here, studying under your tutelage and trusting that you are leading them in the right way, teaching them the proper way to worship God. But they do not worship God. Rather, they worship these many books of tradition and the false teachers who wrote them. All day long they pore over these books—false writings by false teachers. It is my duty, as one who believes in the true and living God, to show them—and you—the right way to worship God according to the Holy Bible. This is my duty before God and all people. And so, that is who I am—one who wants to lead you to true faith in the living God."

The teacher then asked, "How did you come to speak on the subject of Christ? Do you know who He is?" I replied, "The trouble here is in the language. I say 'Christ,' but you say in Hebrew, 'Messiah.' He is the one in whom you claim to believe, and all day long His name is on your lips: 'Messiah'—Christ. They are one and the same person. Now you see that this one who for you has been, up to this moment, unknown is now known. You have learned the first small part about faith in the Messiah, faith in Christ. If you like, we can continue in the Hebrew language only. Then we can speak freely about Yeshua—Jesus—Salvation. These things I am telling you are not taken from books of false teachings but from the Holy Bible itself, and you can see it for yourself right here, in black and white." The teacher was visibly shaken and excused himself, saying he had no more time to talk with me. Then he left.

I was sad that at this special time of year, when the Light of Life came into the world, this teacher and his students are still living in deep darkness. I pray that I will have further opportunities to speak with them. Then, perhaps some year they too will be able to sing from their hearts, "Joy to the world! The Lord is come."

—1997

# KILLING TIME

Once every two months, I must take my wife to the hospital for a checkup on her eye following her cornea transplant surgery. Every time we go, there is a long line of people, and we must wait patiently for her turn. People are always looking at their watches, and some are not as patient as others.

We have met some very interesting people at the hospital—people from many walks of life. The last time we were there, two Russian priests approached me and asked if the seats next to us were free. "Yes," I responded, and because they spoke Russian, they were pleased to learn that I too spoke that language. We immediately began conversing, and our discussion quickly turned to the matter of faith. They were very sure of themselves and showed me their books of commentary, which they were positive contained the root of faith. Although they were Russian priests, they reminded me of the many Ultra-Orthodox Jews I have spoken to over the years— trusting in the words of man rather than in the living Word of God.

I showed them my small Bible and asked, "Which book is of

greater value?" They answered, "We don't want to see anything in Hebrew because we don't speak that language." I replied, "If you like, I will give you a complete translation of any passage in this book." Then I asked, "Have you ever heard about the Bible?" "Oh yes. Do you have a copy with you?" they asked. To their surprise, I told them that the little book I held in my hand was indeed the Holy Bible.

There were many people in the waiting room that day, and as the time wore on, they were looking for ways to kill time. Some of them were new immigrants from Russia. Happy to hear a conversation in their own language, some of them joined in. When we began to speak about Jesus Christ, the priests were sure they were in their own element, but that was their big mistake. I told them, "We must believe in Jesus Christ, not according to the books of commentary that you have, but according to the Bible only. This book alone shows us the right way to come to the Lord. All other books come from false beliefs and superstitions."

The new immigrants listened attentively to our conversation, and most of them agreed that true faith in God comes only according to the Bible. The priests said, "We don't believe what they say." Then I told them, "This is not the belief of Jews only. For the millions of genuine Christians—people who truly believe in Christ—the most important book is the Bible."

These people are walking in darkness because they have never found the true way to faith in Christ. It was not a surprise to me when one of the priests asked, "How did you, a Jew, come to believe in Christ?" I replied, "I can tell from your question how blind you are; you don't even know from which people the Lord Jesus came. Again, if you want to know the truth, you must look to the Bible, not your books full of old, fictitious stories."

Of course, they wanted to know where in the Bible it was written that Jesus was Jewish. I said, "Moses spoke of the Lord Jesus coming from the Jewish people." I opened my Bible to Deuteronomy 18 and read verses 15 and18: "The LORD thy God will raise up unto thee [the Jewish people] a Prophet from the midst of thee, of thy brethren, like unto me; unto him ye shall hearken…I will raise them [the Jewish people] up a Prophet from among their brethren, like unto thee, and will put my words in his mouth, and he shall speak unto them all that I shall command him." I continued, "You see, the Bible gives a clear explanation of Christ's earthly heritage—something you have never read in your many books or heard from your false teachers. The Bible is the root of our faith, not your books."

After further conversation, one of the immigrants said, "Everything you have said is very nice, but we don't understand how a Jew can be so faithful to another religion—a religion that does not belong to the Jewish people." Now I had more opposition, but I responded, "It is good that you have listened to our conversation. I know that you call yourselves good Jews because you follow the old rabbinical traditions of the *Halacha*, but take a good look at the Holy Bible and see what the Lord truly wants from us. He wants us to obey His commandments. And how can we do that? Whom should we follow? Those who have lost their direction?

"Again, I ask you to look at the Bible. It is the true Word of God, and in it we read of the faith of our fathers—Abraham, Isaac, and Jacob—and the words of our prophets. Unfortunately, this book has been hidden from you in Russia for a very long time. Even here in Israel, you are only told about the Old Testament. But if you would study that carefully—especially Isaiah 53, which is never read in the synagogues—you would see for yourselves that it speaks of Jesus Christ."

They were very surprised. "What?" they exclaimed. "Our Holy Scriptures teach about Jesus Christ? That is impossible!" I replied, "It is very possible; in fact, it is more than possible—it is the truth." I then read Isaiah 53—the entire chapter—and explained very clearly what it meant.

What a wonderful opportunity this was to open the blind eyes of these new immigrants, as well as those of the Russian priests. And it all took place in a hospital waiting room, where we sat for more than two hours waiting for my wife to see the doctor. When it was finally her turn and we got up to go into the examining room, one of the men said, "If you have time, we would like to continue this conversation." And so, after my wife's examination was finished, I spoke with these people for another half hour.

I pray that the two Russian priests and the new immigrants were listening, not just with their physical ears, but with their spiritual ears as well. I trust that I will have the opportunity to meet with them again some day and continue our discussion about faith in the Lord Jesus Christ. As it is written in Isaiah 9:2, "The people that walked in darkness have seen a great light; they that dwell in the land of the shadow of death, upon them hath the light shined."

—1998

## FIFTY YEARS...AND COUNTING

This year we are celebrating 50 years since our Declaration of Independence in 1948, which created the modern State of Israel. It seems like only yesterday. But, with the Declaration of Independence came a declaration of war. I was a new immigrant at the time, having come to Israel after passing through the horrors of the Holocaust in Europe. I came here hoping to make a new life for myself after losing my entire family in Hitler's gas chambers.

Only days after I arrived in Israel, following several months in an internment camp on Cyprus, eight Arab countries attacked us—just a tiny nation with a population of a half million souls, most of them Holocaust survivors like myself. Like it or not, we were involved in a whole new set of troubles.

With the memories of the cruel Nazi regime so fresh in our minds, we were thrust into a new Holocaust, a new destruction. Our enemies were so sure of themselves that they did not think they would even have to fight against us because of our small number. They planned a triumphal march through the city of Jerusalem to show the world their great power over little Israel. Were they triumphant? Of course not! In fact, they experienced a crushing defeat. They came against us with millions of men and their best weapons, but they failed.

At that time, I did not know the Lord, and I, along with all the other new Israelis, was reveling in our victory. Then one day I was given a Bible, the first one I had owned in my life. As I began to read it, I soon came upon the account in 1 Samuel 17 of King David's great victory over the Philistine hero, Goliath. I then realized that in 1948, little Israel was just like the little shepherd boy before the giant. Goliath said to David, "Am I a dog, that thou comest to me with staves [sticks]?" (1 Sam. 17:43). I remembered that we had gone against our Arab enemies with nothing more than sticks, compared to their sophisticated weapons. I realized that, just as the Lord had won David's battle over Goliath, the Lord Himself had won little Israel's battle over those eight Arab countries that attacked us. As it is written in Isaiah 49:25, "But thus saith the LORD...I will contend with him that contendeth with thee, and I will save thy children." And again in Psalm 124:2-3, "If it had not been the LORD who was on our side, when men rose up against us; Then they had swallowed us up alive, when their wrath was kindled against us."

Even today, many people in Israel are sure that it was because we were so strong that we were able to defeat our enemies in 1948—and again and again down through the years. But I stand as a living testimony to all that the Lord has done for us in the many wars we have fought since we have been a nation. I served as a soldier on active duty defusing land mines from 1948 to 1973 and have witnessed the many miracles the Lord has performed for us. We never could have defeated our enemies in our own strength. That is why even now, 50 years after our independence, people still must be told who was on our side—and has promised to be on our side forever.

A few weeks ago, some students from a nearby high school came to my home and asked me to tell them about the War of Independence. They explained that they had received a homework assignment requiring them to interview a veteran of that war. I was happy to cooperate, and so they asked me many questions, but the most important in their minds was, "How could it be that such a small nation made such a great victory?" In answer, I opened my Bible and read Deuteronomy 7:17-18: "If thou shalt say in thine heart, These nations are more than I; how can I dispossess them? Thou shalt not be afraid of them, but shalt well remember what the LORD thy God did unto Pharaoh, and unto all Egypt."

As we spoke, the students wrote and wrote in their notebooks, and the interview lasted more than two hours. I explained to them that we did not achieve this great victory in the way in which they had been taught in school—through our own power. No! In 1948, we were a destroyed people—physically and emotionally—having gone through the terrible Holocaust. Most of us had not learned to speak Hebrew, since the war erupted within weeks and even days of our arrival in Israel, so we had difficulty even communicating with one another. I then showed them pictures of the old weapons Israel used in the war of 1948. I told them, "They were nothing compared to the powerful weapons the Arabs used against us. So, I ask you, who was on our side? Were we that strong? Of course not. We were, as the Lord said in Isaiah 41:14, nothing more than a 'worm.' " Then I read to them Isaiah 41:8-15, showing them that in spite of our small size and lack of weapons, the Lord fought for us then, as He has done down through the millennia and right up to today.

Then, slowly, we came around to the subject of faith in God. They asked, "Why do you speak so much about the Bible?" I said, "It is impossible to speak about war without looking at the living facts in God's Word about the great things the Lord has done for us. Take a good look at 1 Samuel 17 and you will see that without the

Lord's help, King David, who was only a child at the time, could not have gone against a beast like Goliath. But what did David say to him? 'Thou comest to me with a sword, and with a spear, and with a shield; but I come to thee in the name of the LORD of hosts, the God of the armies of Israel, whom thou hast defied' [1 Sam. 17:45]. It is the same with Israel today. We stand before our enemies, who are as numerous as a plague of locusts, not in our own strength. No, we are not heroes. If you do not say in your report that the Lord was on our side, you will be lying to yourselves and to everyone else."

These young students, who before were far away from the Bible in their thinking, then asked if I would give them a Bible, and I was happy to do so. I pray that as they read it, the Lord will open their eyes to the truth and they will see Him as the great Defender of His Chosen People, Israel.

And so, 50 years have passed since I came to this land. And what has happened to me here? The Lord has protected and spared me through many battles, through difficulties on the job, through serious illness, and through innumerable dangers. He has given me a wonderful wife, four wonderful children, and eleven wonderful grandchildren (and soon there will be two more). He has provided all our needs through the years, as we have depended on Him. But, most important of all, He saved my soul. As I read that little black Bible given to me by a dear lady on a street in Jerusalem after the 1948 war, I confessed my sins before Him and accepted Him as my Messiah and Savior. Since then I have had the great privilege of being His servant here in His Holy Land. I have spoken to multitudes of people—people of all ages, nationalities, and religions. Some have accepted the Lord as their Messiah and Savior, some have not, and some are still undecided. I pray that He will give me many more years to serve Him in this great battle for the souls of my brethren according to the flesh.

—1998